*I*NTERACTIVE MATHS TEACHING IN THE PRIMARY SCHOOL

York
Information

APR 2023

INTERACTIVE MATHS TEACHING IN THE PRIMARY SCHOOL

Nick Pratt

P·C·P

Paul Chapman Publishing

First published 2006

Apart from any fair dealing for the purposes of research or private study, or criticism or review, as permitted under the Copyright, Designs and Patents Act, 1988, this publication may be reproduced, stored or transmitted in any form, or by any means, only with the prior permission in writing of the publishers, or in the case of reprographic reproduction, in accordance with the terms of licences issued by the Copyright Licensing Agency. Enquiries concerning reproduction outside those terms should be sent to the publishers.

 Paul Chapman Publishing
A SAGE Publications Company
1 Oliver's Yard
55 City Road
London EC1Y 1SP

SAGE Publications Inc
2455 Teller Road
Thousand Oaks, California 91320

SAGE Publications India Pvt Ltd
B-42, Panchsheel Enclave
Post Box 4109
New Delhi 110 017

Library of Congress Control Number: 2006904536

A catalogue record for this book is available from the British Library

ISBN-10 1-4129-2041-8   ISBN-13 978-1-4129-2041-4
ISBN-10 1-4129-2042-6   ISBN-13 978-1-4129-2042-1 (pbk)

Typeset by Pantek Arts Ltd, Maidstone, Kent
Printed in Great Britain by the Cromwell Press, Trowbridge, Wiltshire
Printed on paper from sustainable resources

CONTENTS

ACKNOWLEDGEMENTS

My thanks go to the many teachers and student teachers who have worked with me so willingly and who have offered me so much to think about. It is this thinking that has provided the impetus and material for this book, and which has made coming to work so enjoyable. My thanks also to my father, George, who dropped everything to 'hatchet' the drafts and help me write more clearly.

ABOUT THE AUTHOR

Nick Pratt has worked at the Faculty of Education of the University of Plymouth for 12 years and, before that, taught in schools in Exeter. His degree was originally in Engineering but, more recently, he gained his PhD which was focused on how teachers and children interact in primary mathematics classrooms. Having worked with teacher training students on undergraduate and PGCE routes, he now works on the University's Integrated Masters Programme delivering CPD to teachers across the South-West of England.

Nick lives with his wife and three children in Exmouth, Devon where the sea and the sun are constant reminders that life, both at home and at work, should be enjoyed.

CHAPTER 1

What this book is about ... and how to use it

This chapter will ...

■ introduce what this book is about and set the context for it in terms of the kind of mathematics curriculum that we have in schools;

■ introduce some of the dilemmas that characterise teachers' teaching of this curriculum;

■ explain how the book is laid out and what each chapter addresses.

Introduction

Teaching has become a complicated business. More precisely, it has become complicated *and* it has become a business. National strategies for mathematics and for literacy (subsequently superseded by overarching National Primary and Key Stage 3 strategies); interactive whiteboards; higher level teaching assistants; individual targets for every child, not to mention performance management for teachers themselves; league tables; and the whole shebang managed and made accountable through a raft of requirements from central government. Meanwhile, this profusion of initiatives has created the climate for an army of consultants, advisors and inspectors, all of whom are ready, at the drop of a cheque book, to tell us the real secret of 'raising standards' – though standards of what often seems less clear.

In this book I consider mathematics, how it is learnt, and hence how teaching might best take place. In particular, I focus on how teachers may teach 'interactively' with the whole class – one of the key approaches promoted by recent national strategies. I should add, though, that we cannot understand whole class teaching separate from other aspects of teaching, and so whilst it is the main focus, I also discuss approaches to group work, task setting and other aspects of the maths teacher's job.

Although, as I write, the National Numeracy Strategy in primary schools is gradually being superseded by new foci at primary level, many of its essential elements seem here to stay and have been extended into secondary schools. Interaction, especially with the whole class, is certainly one of these elements. As you will see, I want to consider some of the very real benefits that the strategy and other initiatives have brought with them. However, I also want to clear away some of the debris that they have left behind, and to challenge some of the rhetoric that they have introduced. In doing so, my aim is to try to rethink, and thereby make more useful, the advice that has been offered to teachers in such vast quantities over recent years.

Three premises underpin what I have to say. The first is that teaching is, and always should be, an essentially straightforward affair. Note that this is not to claim that it is always easy, nor to deny the considerable skill needed by the teacher and learner. Rather, it should be straightforward in the sense that, underlying all the complexity that we may choose to impose on it, learning fundamentally involves *people communicating about ideas with each other*. Communication, largely through language, making use of symbols to represent concepts, allows us to make sense of our world in ways that other animals can only dream of – were they, that is, able to dream that way. It is through such communication – both verbal and non-verbal – that learning mainly takes place and, though in some individuals this communication is impaired, for most of us it is a readily available, and continuously employed, resource in our daily lives. As Gordon Wells (1987, p. 222) points out 'we are the meaning makers – every one of us: children, parents and teachers. To try to make sense, to construct stories, and to share them with others in speech and writing is an essential part of being human'.

My second premise is this. Whilst we can make the act of teaching and learning as complicated as we like, there is a basic truth which underpins it: *children will learn more effectively if they think more deeply*. We give children 'work' to do, usually in the form of tasks to carry out. But these tasks are not the end product. Rather, they are containers within which thinking can take place; the means by which we can engage children in thinking, using language, about an issue of importance. Tasks can engender talking/thinking activity. They can be planned or spontaneous, complex or straightforward, individual or grouped, make use of pencils or PCs, but if they do not serve this basic function of challenging children to think anew then they are unlikely to be effective in allowing them to develop new meaning.

My final premise relates to the meaning of *theory* and *practice*, and to the interrelationship between the two. Some years ago I was asked by the deputy head teacher of a local independent school to do two INSET sessions on numeracy. As we negotiated what I might do he made very clear to me that the teachers 'didn't want any theory; just practical ideas'. Presumably, he meant that the staff did not want me to recount, at great length, the ideas of others, perhaps as they appear in books, and that the teachers only wanted to know *what* to do and *how* to do it.

A moment's thought shows the danger of this notion. However clearly and accurately I can describe how to act, each person carries out these actions as part of *their* ongoing life and every action we take is loaded with, and affected by, the meanings and associations of past experiences. It is these meanings and associations that I call theory, and the term therefore refers to *the ideas one has about actions*. Note that these can be implicit, but that making them explicit is likely to allow you to consider them more fully and to make choices about your actions.

Above all, schools carry with them very particular meanings, with each person in that context taking up his or her own 'position' in the social milieu. No two actions will be the same when carried out in different classrooms, or at different times. This becomes significant when we try to implement recommended teaching approaches, in the form of instructions for how to act as teachers. Recommendations, like children's work tasks, are merely vehicles for meaning and do not hold meaning independently of the context within which they are carried out. Practice (one's actions) cannot then be separated from theory (the meaning one associates with actions); actions always both relate to past experiences and imply future experiences for all participants.

Note the change to the meaning of theory here; no longer just the decontextualised ideas of others, but now your own ideas, as well as those of others, relating to the teaching situations you are exposed to. Asking 'what's the theory behind this?' need not imply any reference to other people's thinking; it can simply mean 'what is making me act this way (and is it a good idea)?'.

On the other hand, education research has provided many insights into just the kinds of questions that we might want to ask of our own practice and it would be foolish to ignore the wealth of information it offers. One of the aims of this book, then, is to attempt to use some of this research to help the reader evaluate his or her own practice. In particular, it takes the recommendations of recent curriculum initiatives relating to *whole class interactive teaching* and supports the reader in asking why, and exactly how, one might act this way. Before focusing in on interaction though, I begin with a more general perspective on changes to the mathematics curriculum as a whole as a way of laying out the ground.

Curriculum change

Looking back over the last twenty-five years, three key national initiatives stand out. First, *Mathematics Counts*, known commonly as the Cockcroft report (DES, 1982), illuminated clearly some of the limitations of (then) current practice and made wide-ranging and informed recommendations for change. The quality of the work carried out by the committee, under W.H. Cockcroft, is apparent in the frequency with which the final report is still referred to today. To put this conjecture to the test, I have just reached for my copy of the report and looked up *mental mathematics*, the first thing that came to mind. Paragraph 315 immediately refers to the idea that:

> *We refer in this section to 'mental mathematics' rather than 'mental calculation' because we wish to include within our discussion both the mental calculation and also the oral work which should play an important part in the teaching of primary mathematics.*

Similarly the very next section notes that 'young children should not be allowed to move too quickly to written work in mathematics' (paragraph 316). Neither of these quotations would look out of place in current curriculum circulars and as one reads on, the text is packed with well thought-out advice, about such matters as:

■ *mental rehearsal* ('the more that such rehearsal can increase links with the existing network [of facts], the more effective it is likely to be' – paragraph 237);

■ *mental calculation* ('… [it is a] now well established fact that those who are mathematically effective in daily life seldom make use "in their heads" of the standard written methods which are taught in classrooms' – paragraph 256); and

■ discussion ('… much of the value [of work] will be lost unless the work which has been done, and the results which have been obtained, are discussed with the children so as to establish the necessary concepts' – paragraph 286), the term 'plenary' not yet being in circulation, of course!

The profound effect of the Cockcroft report on mathematics education thinking was reflected in the second significant publication, the National Curriculum (DES, 1989). Not only was the content of the curriculum detailed for all schools, but enshrined in this content were many of the recommendations from Cockcroft seven years earlier. Most significantly, the way that children should both 'use and apply' their mathematics, developing understanding *in the process*, was outlined in a specific programme of study. Alongside the statutory curriculum document, 'non-statutory guidance' discussed pedagogy in some detail, laying out how the mathematical content could be operationalised through teaching. Again, Cockcroft's influence resonated throughout and the curriculum included the statutory requirement that children develop flexible, mental mathematical methods, both *through* and *for* the solution of problems.

Despite the wisdom of both the Cockcroft report and the National Curriculum with its guidance, there remained a dual difficulty for teachers. First, though they discussed approaches to teaching at a general level, neither document told teachers more specifically what to *do*. Indeed, Cockcroft's committee noted that 'we are aware that there are some teachers who would wish us to indicate a definitive style for the teaching of mathematics, but we do not believe that this is either desirable or possible' (DES, 1989, paragraph 242) and the non-statutory guidance of the National Curriculum dealt mainly with practice at the level of school policy.

Second, even early versions of the curriculum document (e.g. DFE, 1995) and its guidance required teachers to teach children to 'develop flexible methods of working with number, orally and mentally' (p. 3), but did not detail what this meant in mathematical terms. What was a flexible method? How did one develop them? How did they relate to written work and to standardised procedures on paper? These were all questions that the National Curriculum raised, but failed to answer in detail.

This double dilemma for teachers was resolved, at least superficially, by the National Numeracy Strategy (NNS) for primary schools. The vast majority of teachers welcomed its introduction because 'finally' there was clear advice about exactly what to do in the classroom (a definitive style, promoted and validated through official guidance and the inspection regime) and about precisely what children needed to know in order to calculate effectively in their heads. In addition, it was all based, teachers were assured (Brown et al., 2000), on 'what works', an authoritative set of practices which had been shown to make a difference to outcomes in children's test scores. Whatever one thinks about this, undoubtedly, no other curriculum initiative has had such a profound effect as the NNS on teaching practices.

The National Strategy: a change for the better?

The National Numeracy Strategy at Key Stages 1 and 2, and later the Key Stage 3 National Strategy, appeared to fill a hole left open by previous curriculum initiatives. For the first time, teachers had clear instruction regarding both what to teach and how to teach it, and the *Framework for Teaching Mathematics* (DFEE, 1999a) with its term-by-term plans and examples of exactly what to teach seemed to make the life of the teacher easier in many ways. Certainly, it tightened up control of what was being learnt, when and how. But, for all the increased structure and control over the curriculum, indeed perhaps because of it, other dilemmas have emerged for teachers.

To begin to explore these dilemmas I invite you to engage in a few minutes thought. I could have called this a 'task' for you, the reader, to carry out, but the word 'task' has particular connotations in English associated with onerous duty. Furthermore, I cannot know the extent, or manner, of your engagement, or what you will learn as a result. As I hope you will understand as you read further, these points are central to the issues that this book aims to address – the way in which the quality of interaction with a class of children is highly dependent on the human relationships involved. What follows is therefore an invitation to stop and think and, I hope, an opportunity to develop your own 'theory' in relation to teaching. The invitations can be declined of course – though you will miss the opportunity that I hope they present.

STOP AND THINK

The following list is taken from the non-statutory guidance that accompanied the original National Curriculum for Mathematics in 1989 (NCC, 1989, pp. B8-B9). It lists the features that, it claims, an effective mathematics scheme of work 'should take into account'.

For each feature listed:

▶ decide on the extent to which the scheme of work you currently use takes account of the feature;

▶ consider the pros and cons of your decisions for both teaching and learning.

- Activities should bring together different areas of mathematics.

- The order of activities should be flexible.

- Activities should be balanced between tasks which develop knowledge, skills and understanding, and those which develop the ability to tackle practical problems.

- Activities should be balanced between the applications of mathematics and ideas which are purely mathematical.

- Activities should be balanced between those which are short in duration and those which have scope for development over an extended period of time.

- Activities should, where appropriate, use pupils' own interests or questions either as starting points or as further lines of development.

- Activities should, where appropriate, involve both independent and cooperative work.

- Tasks should be both of the kind which have an exact result or answer and those which have many possible outcomes.

- Activities should be balanced between different modes of learning: doing, observing, talking and listening, discussing with other pupils, reflecting, drafting, reading and writing etc.

The effects of curriculum change are clearly complex and multifaceted. Though recent national strategies have brought with them greater detail regarding curriculum content (particularly in relation to calculations) they have not removed other, fundamental, dilemmas for teachers. Moreover, research carried out since their introduction is beginning to point to some limitations, not just in the stated aims of improving standardised test scores, but also in terms of wider considerations such as the depth and security of children's engagement in the learning process (Alexander, 2000; Brown et al., 2003; Burns and Myhill, 2004; Hardman et al., 2003).

The chapters that follow argue that the highly structured approach to teaching advocated by current educational initiatives tends to create a systemic tension for teachers. This tension revolves around the extent to which teaching should, on the one hand, provide the freedom for children to make sense of their mathematics together through discussion and reflection whilst, on the other hand, controlling what is learned and being accountable for it. Tight control affords teachers many advantages in a world of accountability – but it also mitigates against many of the things that characterise what it is to think, and act, like a mathematician. The book addresses these issues, taking as its focus the notion of 'interactive teaching': what this means, what it offers and what challenges it presents.

Structure and use of the book

This introductory chapter has laid out some of the background and the key ideas of the book. In **Chapter 2** I go on to look at *interaction*, exploring what this phrase might mean. One observation here is that official documentation is not at all clear regarding the rationale for using this approach, which sets up the need to develop some kind of theoretical perspective for its use in teaching mathematics. This, in turn, prompts the need to be clear about what we mean by *mathematics*, and some consideration is given to the nature of the subject, therefore.

Chapter 3 explores how talking together in a mathematical setting can be used effectively for understanding mathematics. Importantly though, it is not just the act of talking that counts. Rather, the intent behind the talk – the reason for talking – is vital and so I introduce the idea of a classroom *discourse*, meaning the practices, norms and expectations of the classroom, of which talk is one part. The chapter explores how, in theory at least, one can engineer purposeful talk with a whole class.

Chapters 4 and 5 then move the discussion from the theoretical level to the practical, exploring, respectively, the challenges of using whole class talk in the classroom and some practical suggestions for overcoming the challenges. These ideas are then illustrated in **Chapters 6 and 7**, in which I offer some suggested starting points for more effective interaction. The former chapter deals with numerical examples whilst the latter takes shape and space as its focus.

It should be apparent that the book becomes more practically orientated as it moves on. Readers could, therefore, dip into the ideas presented in Chapters 6 and 7 and try them out in their own classrooms. However, this might miss the wider point of the book, which is based on the assertion that whilst national strategies for mathematics have told teachers *what* to do, they have not offered sufficient insight into *how* to do it. Ironically, the earlier initiatives outlined above – the Cockcroft report and the National Curriculum with its non-statutory guidance – were criticised for their lack of clarity about exactly what to do in practice. In attempting to rectify this however, the national strategies have not solved the problem. If, as I suggested above, theory is linked to teachers' experiences and mathematical identities, which are linked in turn to the context in which they work, then so are their practices. Put simply, one person's 'demonstration', 'interaction' or 'plenary' is not like another's precisely because these actions are not independent of the context in which they are carried out. We do not demonstrate 'to' people, we demonstrate 'in relation to' them; and in relation to all the other aspects of the context such as physical environment and social norms and expectations. Cockcroft's assertion that a 'definitive style' is neither desirable nor possible appears to show great wisdom – though it seems almost heretical too in an age where 'evidence-based practice' and accountability are so dominant. The book aims to unpick, therefore, the implicit and hidden aspects of interactive teaching and this relies, in turn, on an understanding of the issues involved – and a more complete reading.

Chapter 8 brings the book together and aims to help the reader to audit his or her own practice in terms of the ideas that have been addressed, as well as encouraging and supporting the idea of further exploration of the issues through small scale research in teachers' own classrooms. This may be particularly useful for mathematics coordinators who want to plan school INSET.

Though intended to be practical, the book is also meant to be aspirational – in the sense that it deliberately challenges some of the standard things that we tend to do as teachers and presents, what I anticipate are, interesting alternatives that we might begin to try. However you read it, I hope that the book offers you something fresh in terms of an insight into your classroom and how your interaction with children is supporting their learning of mathematics.

CHAPTER 2

Interactive teaching and the primary mathematics curriculum

This chapter will …

■ introduce the idea that an approach to teaching maths based on tight objectives might be problematic for teachers;

■ discuss the meaning of 'interactive' and identify some initial implications for the classroom;

■ explore the importance of understanding the subject well, particularly its 'essence'.

For some readers it may come as a surprise that learning to teach interactively with the whole class, encouraging children to explore different approaches to calculations, was, not so long ago, an exciting and novel challenge for many teachers. Anyone who joined the profession prior to 1998 was probably brought up on a diet of small-group work and individualised textbook schemes. Little emphasis was placed on developing mathematical ideas with the whole class together. Though this is now common practice, not all teachers understand in the same way what it means to teach interactively to the whole class, allowing children freedom to express their own ideas about mathematical issues, even though there have been many attempts to describe it clearly in official documents and training.

Two key ideas underpin the mathematics curriculum as it now stands, in contrast to previous recommendations:

1 a highly detailed and structured approach to calculation, putting mental work at its forefront;

2 considerable teaching of the whole class and the use of more talk, making mathematics a more mental/oral activity than in the past.

Curriculum tensions

In order to help teachers to adapt their teaching to reflect the two key ideas above, numerous training materials have been developed for teachers. The majority of these are probably best described as tightly focused, with specific suggestions regarding what should be done and said by the trainer. The intention has been to ensure that every teacher has had access to the same training, and the result is a set of materials that are very prescriptive in style and designed for use by even the most inexperienced 'tutor'. This has led to a situation in which teachers have been discouraged from too much freedom to interpret ideas for themselves. For example, in the original training materials for the NNS, each 'discussion' was followed by a summary overhead with instructions to the tutor that 'the last action will be to show this overhead and highlight the key points with everyone' (DfEE, 1999b). This kind of practice brings to mind the story of Henry Ford who, it is claimed, assured consumers that one could buy his Model T automobile in any colour one liked … as long as it was black!

A second, and more fundamental, feature of many training materials has been the focus on ideas at the level of practice rather than any attempt to address the underlying principles from which they came. For example, 'effective *teaching*' has been characterised, but without explicit reference made to any theory regarding how learning takes place. Similarly, features of what teachers should 'do' are often described, but without exploring the criteria that would make it appropriate to carry out these actions at any one moment (when, for example, it was better to choose to 'demonstrate and model' than to 'question and discuss').

The thrust, then, of these training materials appears not to have been to engage teachers in fundamental questions regarding 'why', but rather to instruct them in instrumental issues of 'how'. Teachers have been asked to do things in their classrooms without necessarily developing an appropriate theoretical framework to fall back on. Remember of course, in saying this, how in Chapter 1 we defined theory for the purposes of this book. The essential point is that to develop your teaching it helps to be able to articulate why you are doing something in the first place.

It is my belief that the rather instrumental approach to teachers' professional development outlined above has led to a tension in practice. On the one hand the main message has been to encourage children to take ownership over thinking about mathematics, to evolve personal mathematical methods, make their own links between ideas and contribute to a class debate. In learning how to do this, teachers themselves have been encouraged to observe 'leading teachers' in identified schools and to discuss classroom practices.

On the other hand, teachers are now asked to direct what children learn, teach the whole class simultaneously about a single idea and assess exactly what has been learnt so as to address common misunderstandings. Correspondingly, training itself has directed teachers in terms of the key things to 'know' and what 'best practice' should look like.

I am making the assertion here that recent curriculum change has presented teachers with mixed messages about teaching and learning. This applied both to the classroom work with children and to their own learning about using the Strategy. You might think of a hypothetical spectrum in this respect, like that shown overleaf.

At one end:

- Teaching is an activity based on certainty.

- There is a 'right way' to do things which leads to new knowledge being transferred to children.

- Outcomes can be predicted and controlled.

- Teaching has an air of *technicism* about it – teachers merely have to 'do the right thing' and this will guarantee praticular products.

- Teaching dominates with learning subordinate to it.

At the other end:

- Teaching is recognised as uncertain.

- There is no 'right way' because each context is culturally different.

- Learning takes place through negotiation and outcomes for each child will be different, even if they 'do' the same thing.

- Particular outcomes cannot be guaranteed and teachers can only provide the *opportunity* for particular ideas to be developed.

- Teaching is led by the learning needs at any one time.

IN YOUR CLASSROOM

▶ Do you recognise yourself at one end or the other, or in the middle?

▶ Think particularly about:

    ■ why you structure your lessons the way you do;

    ■ where your objectives come from;

    ■ questions you ask;

    ■ explanations you give;

    ■ the opportunity you provide for children to talk;

    ■ the extent to which the children can alter the direction of a lesson.

▶ Do you feel any tensions in your work? If so, what are they?

What does 'interactive' really mean?

In being required to reach certain outcomes from teaching, yet to teach interactively so that children have the chance to develop their own mathematical ideas and approaches, teachers may well find themselves in a tension that is difficult to resolve. The word *interactive* itself is part of this, and what it means to teach interactively needs some thought. Before presenting my ideas, you might like to take some time to consider your own view of the meaning of the word 'interactive'.

STOP AND THINK STOP

▶ On a scale of 'not at all' to 'definitely', decide which of these activities are 'interactive' and which are not.

1 Looking at objects

2 Making things

3 Listening to someone talk

4 Tasting things

5 Reading a book

6 Playing a musical instrument

7 Conversation

8 Writing on a computer

9 Completing a tax return form

10 Making lecture notes

▶ How might you interpret the idea of 'interactive teaching'?

If you stopped to do the thinking above then you should have begun to articulate what *interactive* means to you. You might have considered physical touch and/or the ability to respond to other participants (human or non-human), or perhaps you focused on the *effect* of the activity – sometimes reading is interactive, whilst at other times it is quite passive. Looking at the word interactive itself may help too. Inter-active implies 'causing/producing action between'. Seen this way, anything that causes action to take place between people, or between an object and a person, might be deemed interactive. Importantly, 'interactive teaching' would then become teaching which encourages (or at least allows) action to take place between participants (teachers and/or children, in the case of the classroom).

KEY IDEAS

■ Interacting implies an intent to affect other people's ideas and a willingness to (re)consider your own ideas.

■ Nothing is interactive *per se* therefore. It depends on *how* you go about it.

Considering the root of the word like this suggests that interaction may refer largely to an *effect between* participants – 'participants' here meaning objects or machines, such as books or computers, as well as people. This implies that interaction is as much a state of mind as a physical action; an intent within an act, rather than merely the act itself.

Returning to the list of activities in the last opportunity to 'stop and think', with this notion of interaction in mind, we can see that the activity itself is not the crucial issue, but rather it is the manner in which it is carried out. When I look at an object I can do so in several ways. I can simply stare passively at it or I can look actively with the intent to understand its construction perhaps, or to notice new details about it. Similarly, I can taste things in different ways. Drinking wine is a good example here; often I open a bottle and simply consume it for a fairly immediate taste sensation and its alcoholic effect. At other times I interact with the taste more deliberately, particularly if it is a new wine to me, in which case I am consciously opening myself up to a consideration of tastes and smells and using my memory of previous similar events to evaluate the experience. It is even better if the interaction can be extended to another person tasting the wine with me. The range of experiences, and the opportunity for new ideas to consider therefore, is greater, particularly if the other person is more of an expert than me, a relative wine novice.

PRACTICAL EXAMPLE

Jo, a PGCE student, is working with a Year 5 class. The children have been doing scale drawings, in pairs, of an imaginary new supermarket as part of a project on their local environment. The idea is for them to think about division and multiplication in the context of scaling. Jo has taken digital photos of the diagrams as they have been drawn and is now projecting these onto the interactive whiteboard for the class to discuss. Jo asks one pair to talk about their diagram, but rather than just explaining what they did, the instruction is to describe something that they think is *unique* about the way they worked. The rest of the class are asked to let them finish and then to discuss with their partner how it compares to what they did. Pairs then comment on whether or not they did the same thing and, in so doing, start to compare different approaches to the work.

I hope you can see that the meaning of interaction I am using here is all about the *intent* of the action between two or more people and/or objects. In Jo's case, the interaction was strong because the task she set the children carried with it the intent to compare and contrast ideas, not just to receive them.

Thinking about interaction this way will help us in understanding our teaching better. Two more key ideas immediately become apparent now.

KEY IDEAS

- Because it is the *intent* behind any action that counts as much as the action itself, interactive teaching is more than just a set of teaching *skills*.

- Since what one intends is often both afforded and constrained by what others think, interaction – and hence interactive teaching – will be affected by the way people *feel* about each other.

Finally, an important implication follows on from these two key ideas, namely that to teach *mathematics* interactively you need to have a good understanding of what you are trying to achieve. This is because you need to understand which forms of intent are useful and which are not; put simply, what *do* you intend to achieve through your teaching? Understanding the nature of mathematics as a subject becomes important therefore, as does understanding the curriculum which is, inevitably, a subset of the subject, representing someone else's view of what is important.

The essence of mathematics

Since the exact nature of mathematics has been debated over several thousands of years by people with more expertise than I will ever have, I am not proposing an in-depth discussion here. Luckily, this need not matter and what I aim for instead is to suggest some of the things that might be considered important in teaching the subject. For those who are interested, further reading is also suggested at the end of the chapter.

I have begun to make the case that interaction is largely to do with intent, and so to teach mathematics interactively means that you need to be aware of what you are intending to achieve. Brown (1999) has pointed out that the curriculum in English schools has not stood still in terms of intent for mathematics. Indeed, the curriculum has swung backwards and forwards in relation to the extent to which mathematics should be about processes and procedures or concept development.

STOP AND THINK 🛑

► What do you think the outcomes of maths teaching should be for children leaving primary school?

► Can you place these outcomes in order of priority?

My own answer to the questions in the thinking opportunity above is to identify at least four intended *outcomes* of primary mathematics teaching, namely:

■ *Pupils' development of mathematical ideas* – involving small identifiable units (such as knowledge of multiplication tables), broader conceptual units (such as an understanding of multiplication more widely) and procedures (such as how to compute the product of two multi-digit numbers).

■ *Pupils' ability and willingness to see relationships between ideas* (*why*, for example, multiplication is commutative – i.e. $7 \times 3 = 3 \times 7$).

■ *Pupils' ability to see the opportunity to use mathematics in problem situations, and to do so successfully* (for example, seeing that having four shirts and three pairs of trousers in my wardrobe means that, mathematically, I can wear 12 different outfits – though fashion may dictate that mathematics may not be the best tool to use here!).

■ *Pupils' adoption of certain mathematical dispositions* (enjoyment, resilience, resourcefulness, intuition etc.).

I am hard pressed to order them – unfair, I know, since I suggested that you might do so. Each seems interdependent on the others.

Brown's point though is that the relative importance of each one is a matter of social history. At different stages we have chosen to focus on some at the expense of others. It might be argued that the school system during the transition from the twentieth to twenty-first centuries has focused heavily on the first of my priorities – the development of ideas. In the main, this has been driven by the assessment system, which places heavy emphasis on knowledge, but does not really address either the use of maths or pupils' feelings towards learning it.

Somewhat ironically, the National Curriculum – teachers' statutory duty in teaching terms – paints a very rounded curriculum picture, particularly in its integration of 'Using and Applying' into each programme of mathematical study. It is made clear that mathematical 'knowledge' is to be developed *through* three essential strands: problem solving, communicating and reasoning. The document makes clear that mathematics is not just something to be learnt; rather it is something to be *done*. As one of my colleagues likes to put it: maths is not a spectator sport!

The point here is that maths is not simply a body of knowledge to be 'taken on' by the learner. It is a human activity, a discipline ('subject') that allows the user to understand the world in a different – though not necessarily better – way. It can be helpful to understanding this by considering three components to learning mathematics, as Figure 2.1 shows.

Learning mathematics involves …

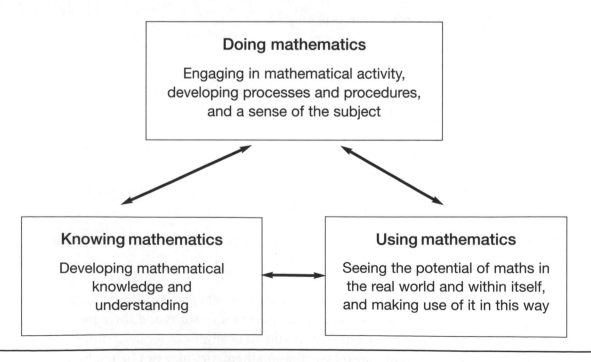

Figure 2.1 **Components of learning mathematics**

In this diagram, the double-headed arrows are crucial, indicating the interrelated nature of these components of learning the subject. Research is beginning to show us that where problem solving is the predominant means of instruction, pupils tend to be both more interested in the subject and also more able to see, and to realise, its potential uses. More importantly, pupils who experience maths in an investigative, problem-based form actually develop *different* mathematics to those children engaged in a more traditional teach-and-practice approach.

It is easy to miss the importance of what I have just stated here: that there is a direct link between the teaching approach and the *nature* of what is learnt (not just the amount that is learnt).

KEY IDEAS

- *How* we teach directly affects not just children's attitudes but also the *form* of knowledge that they develop.

- Children who learn in a climate of enquiry and who engage in problem solving regularly, tend to develop knowledge that is more flexible and can be put to use more readily.

For me, what I think is really important about this is that, rather than simply learning mathematical knowledge and then learning to apply it, it tells us that children need to *be* young mathematicians; to engage in mathematical activity/application and to develop their understanding *from* this.

I want to note immediately that this *does not mean a complete change to all that you might be doing in your classroom*, nor that we need to throw away all our resources and buy a new set. What it does mean though is that our intent towards those resources might change so that everything attempted in the classroom is done within what John Mason has called a 'conjecturing atmosphere' (Sfard et al., 1998).

PRACTICAL EXAMPLE

Judith has realised that whenever her Year 3 children use a worksheet their intent is to complete it, rather than understand it. To change this she gives them a worksheet which she has filled in herself, telling the children that it was done by another child in the same class last year. She has deliberately included some mistakes based on common difficulties her own children are experiencing.

The children's task is then to 'mark' the sheet. More specifically, they have to agree, in their group, what feedback they would give to the child. In particular:

- what was done well and what maths was well understood;

- what the problems might have been;

- how they might help the child.

The task is for each group to prepare a short verbal report ready to give at the plenary.

Mathematics, then, far from being an attempt only to acquire a body of prescribed knowledge, should become an attempt by learners to *explore* the ideas that make up the subject – and to come to know them *through* that exploration. Teachers need to support learners in coming to understand these ideas in new (to them) ways, since this is intrinsically what mathematicians seek to do. The focus should be on the process of exploration, with the coming-to-know as its by-product, not the other way round. Judith achieved this by making 'understanding' the focus of the task; the children had to explore what was going on mathematically.

So, with this view of maths in mind, if it takes three mathematicians to change a light bulb today, tomorrow we might expect them to be working on how to do it with two, one, or then none at all … and very soon they will be considering whether negative mathematicians exist and whether they might be ever more efficient at domestic electrics.

IN YOUR CLASSROOM

Use the diagram in Figure 2.1 to think about your own classroom practice, and consider:

▶ The relative weight of the three components. Are they of equal importance, or does one outweigh the others?

▶ Which of the arrows is strongest. Are they all double-headed?

▶ Whether your teaching moves equally between all three boxes. Does it tend to get stuck in the 'knowing' box?

Before leaving the question of the nature of mathematics, I want to raise one more important issue for teaching it. By way of introduction, let me ask a question: what is a square? You are probably happy to respond that it is 'a four-sided shape with all its sides equal and right angles at each corner', or something along those lines. All well and good, but now let me ask you to find me a square. This time you might point to a ceiling tile, or to a cream cracker. But are these really squares? You would probably give up the cream cracker (rounded corners) but might fight your ground over the ceiling tile. Once I have whipped out my Vernier callipers though, and demonstrated that the sides are not *quite* equal in length, you may have to concede this one too. One might envisage a measurement arms race now as you point to squares which are more and more 'square' and I pull out more and more accurate measuring devices that prove each one to be not quite equal in length or right angular at the corners.

I may be playing games here, but a serious issue emerges. When one asks 'what is a square?', showing me a physical object never does the trick because this is always a *representation* of a square. Note, for example, how, in the paragraph above, I referred to 'squares that were more and more square'. The point here is that a square is *an idea*. And so is 'four', and 'multiplication', and 'triangular numbers'; indeed so are all mathematical objects. This is a point which is, I think, missed by many teachers, and this is a shame since at least two important implications result from it.

First, it validates the whole idea of 'mental' maths – since maths is intrinsically mental in this sense. Put another way, if maths is the study of a set of ideas then thinking seems like a good approach to take to it. In addition, we all need to agree the ideas and to 'mean' the same thing by them, so thinking together and *communicating* about this also seems sensible. Furthermore, although the subject may be made up of ideas, this is not to say that they don't have some 'reality'. The ideas are real, at least in as far as they make sense in relation to each other. Once I have agreed the idea of counting, then addition is out there waiting to be understood. This means that *reasoning* becomes useful in order to *solve the problem* of what it is and how it works. Note, by the way, how the words I have italicised in this paragraph are those that form the basis of the Using and Applying strand of our curriculum. This is not a coincidence!

The second implication is that to complain that maths is *abstract* is to miss the point. Maths *is* abstract; at least in as far as ideas are abstract. That is why it does not work very well on TV, since ideas are hard to see. But, it is its abstract nature that gives maths its power since one is no longer locked into the reality of physical objects. For example, working with three counting blocks may allow me to see the pattern:

3 + 0

2 + 1

1 + 2

0 + 3

as I partition them in different ways. However, it is the ability *to abstract* (note abstract is now a verb) this pattern that allows me to see that ⁻1 + 4, ⁻2 + 5 etc. is implied. And, having abstracted it thus, I can return to the real world via an application and see that owing £2 and having £5 in my wallet means that I effectively have £3.

As Ian Stewart has put it:

> Mathematics is about ideas. In particular it is about the way that different ideas relate to each other. If certain information is known, what else must necessarily follow? The aim of mathematics is to understand such questions by stripping away the inessentials and penetrating to the core of the problem. It is not just a question of getting the right answer; more a matter of understanding why an answer is possible at all, and why it takes the form that it does.

(1996, p. 2)

KEY IDEAS

- ■ Maths is fundamentally about the study of ideas and we use reasoning to do this.

- ■ The purpose of our teaching is to help children to abstract mathematical ideas from the tasks we give them.

Summary

- Allowing children the freedom to contribute ideas and develop idiosyncratic ways of working, whilst simultaneously requiring teachers to reach specific endpoints (objectives) might be seen as a tension.

▶ Do you see this as a tension? How do you balance it up in your classroom?

- Thinking of *interaction* in terms of the *intent* behind actions might be useful. It allows us to see that it is not superficially what we do that counts, but what is *meant* by this action.

▶ How aware are you (becoming) of the intent behind what you do in your maths teaching?

- Mathematics is a human activity in which the goal is exploration of the relationships between ideas. Engagement in problem solving is fundamentally mathematical and working this way changes the kind of learning that children end up with.

▶ If you asked the children in your class what they thought maths was all about, what might they tell you?

📖 Further reading

Askew, M. (2005) 'Sending out an SOS', *Mathematics Teaching*, 192, pp.22–3.

Burns, C. and Myhill, D. (2004) 'Interactive or inactive? A consideration of the nature of interaction in whole class teaching', *Cambridge Journal of Education*, 34(1), 35–49.

Stewart, I. (1996) *From Here to Infinity. A Guide to Today's Mathematics*. Oxford: Oxford University Press.

CHAPTER 3

Making mathematical meaning through talk

This chapter will …

■ discuss what it means to 'understand' mathematics and how this can take place in a classroom setting;

■ introduce the term 'classroom *discourse*' to make sense of how understanding develops through what is *said* (talk), *done* (practices) and, more implicitly, *meant* (via social expectations and norms);

■ aim to develop your personal theory about how discourse works to prepare you to make sense of how your classroom functions.

Why making mathematical meaning?

You might have asked yourself, as you turned the page and saw this chapter, why I did not just call it *understanding mathematics through talk*. Such a question is entirely reasonable. However, in my mind the choice reflects an important point about the nature of *understanding* that underpins much of what I want to say about practice later.

At first sight, the idea that 'understanding' needs any explanation might seem strange. Surely, we know what it means to understand something, or not? What I hope to illustrate though is that things are not as straightforward as they first appear and that an alternative perspective on understanding can help us to see our classrooms in very different, and more importantly, useful ways.

Understanding as 'absolute'

The first issue that I aim to address is the extent to which understanding is *absolute* – by which I mean complete and unchanging. To do so, let me ask a question. Do you understand multiplication? Well, yes, I suspect that everyone reading this book could find the product 5×12; but what about if I ask you to find 0.5×0.0012? And what about $5_8 \times 12_8$ (5_8 and 12_8 being in base 8)? And what about the product of two vectors? And anyway, did you simply compute the answers mechanically, or did you 'understand' what you were doing? The point is quickly made, I hope, that understanding can be thought of as having many dimensions. For example we might imagine ourselves saying all of the following: 'I understand it a bit'; 'I understood that one, but not this one'; 'I don't understand how this one relates to this one'; 'I understood it last week!'.

At one level, all this is obvious. Yet schooling is often organised around principles which imply that understanding is fixed at any one moment. How often, for example, do we find ourselves talking about whether or not 'a child understands'; or reading official documentation which dictates that pupils should be taught to 'understand division' (currently a key objective for Y3); or using test scores as a measure of 'what the child understands'. Of course, this is unfair criticism in many ways, since professionals would rightly argue that these words may simply be shorthand for the more sophisticated meaning of understanding outlined above. The difficulty is that whilst we may intend this to be the case, labels quickly develop which solidify understanding back into the absolute.

KEY IDEA

■ Understanding is relative to time and context, not absolute and permanent.

Where understanding is considered to be an absolute, two important things tend to happen. Firstly, governmental policy has encouraged teachers to set, and to share with the children, learning objectives at the start of lessons. Viewing understanding as either/or (that is the children either understand or do not) may tend to encourage us to drive towards a perceived goal regardless of what happens during the lesson. If there is some*thing* to *be* understood then we simply need to carry on until we reach it. Objectives, in these terms, become *end-points*, towards which we are driving all the children. Alternatively, if understanding is seen as something complex which develops, but is never complete (since every mathematical idea can be linked to further ideas or understood in new ways), then it may be more likely that we plan for a 'rich opportunity' from which children will draw their own learning. Here, objectives may be seen more as *centre-points*, around which the teacher teaches; often exploring other avenues, but usually turning back towards them.

IN YOUR CLASSROOM

▶ How are you and your colleagues using the word 'understanding'? Look for different ways in which it is being used. To what extent is it seen as a fixed commodity or as a shifting one?

▶ How do you view your lesson objectives? Are they 'end-points' or 'centre-points'? Do you teach *at* them, or *around* them?

The second point about a flexible view of 'understanding' is that, after the learning experience, assessing what has 'been understood' is very different from assessing 'how understanding has changed'. The former is more likely to lead to labelling (success/failure to understand) with the focus on superficial aspects of the learning; the latter to a more sophisticated, child-centred consideration of how the child is thinking. Research has consistently shown the second of these to be a key factor in improving teaching (for example, see Black and Wiliam, 1998 from which the idea of *Assessment for Learning* developed).

Whilst these points are significant, a third and perhaps more important point is that for the learner it feels much safer to talk about developing or improving one's understanding, rather than simply understanding or not. The former clearly implies that progress may be slow, that it is alright not to understand at the start, that everyone will have different levels of understanding and so on. The latter simply dumps learners into the able, or unable, groupings – metaphorically or literally.

PRACTICAL EXAMPLE

Emiko is starting a new unit of work on shape and space with her Year 2 children. She begins her carpet discussion by asking:

▶ *'Who can tell me what a square is?'*

Several children put their hands up, but it is all the usual suspects and the children she really wants to know about don't offer anything. She doesn't want to pick on anyone at this stage because she is aware that some of the children find this intimidating and might close up even more.

The next day, when she is widening the discussion to other 2D shapes, she asks a different question:

▶ *'Who can tell me something about triangles? Anything is fine.'*

This time more children put up their hands, including Barry who rarely contributes. Emiko picks him and he tells the class that he played a triangle in assembly last week. It's a small start, but it allows Emiko to build up a discussion by saying: 'That's a good start Barry. Can anyone add anything else?'

Soon the class have built up a good picture of the properties of triangles together, including Barry who has contributed again to the discussion by describing what 'his' triangle looked like.

Note how, in this example, the first question requires *the* answer whilst the second simply seeks responses. Of course, if the children are not used to this kind of request then they will be suspicious at first. If the request for contributions is genuine though, and answers are consistently taken seriously, they will soon get used to the idea that the intent behind the interaction is to build up a strong response together, not as individuals.

Understanding as 'individual'

Seeing the relative, rather than absolute, nature of understanding is fairly straightforward, but a second and perhaps more difficult issue is the extent to which understanding is *individual*? One problem we face is that we are led to believe in understanding as a measurable quality of human beings – understanding is seen as being 'acquired' in varying amounts. This metaphor of personal acquisition is shown in the language that we use, so that people are seen to be 'holding' understanding, 'gaining' knowledge, 'taking things on board' and 'getting to grips with things'. In many ways this is sensible; after all, my brain is processing information and making sense of stimuli. But there is another way to view things.

Consider the way you are reading this book. What are you understanding from it? Indeed, are you actually understanding *from* it; or are you, more accurately, understanding *with* it, or *using* it? Could you be understanding this now if it wasn't for me having written it? Well yes, you could have been spurred into thinking about these ideas by some other means, but whatever this means might be, you remain reliant on some form of interaction with the ideas. What becomes apparent is that every act of understanding is, to varying degrees, related to our *culture* (what we know and what we consider normal, everyday), our *history* (what we have experienced before and what we have made of it) and our *social* setting (including the context within which we are understanding and our relationships with others).

PRACTICAL EXAMPLE

I have been asked by a group of teachers to do some work with them in school about mathematics teaching. I begin to talk about working with the whole class. Each teacher hears what I am saying in relation to his or her own history of teaching. Some younger ones, who have grown up with the National Numeracy Strategy, 'understand' me only in these terms, whilst others, who can remember teaching in different ways, have different understandings of what I mean. This understanding is also affected by the social setting. Some take what I say at face value because I am an expert in their eyes. One woman, though, indignantly defines 'an expert' as simply someone who knows the same as you but lives more than 50 miles away! She feels free to challenge what I am saying. My gender may affect the way people interact with me too, as might my being white and 40 years old.

At the end of the session each person has experienced the same event, but has understood it differently. Furthermore, if I then tested their understanding, what they could say about it would depend on the same factors again; how they are asked, what medium they use to communicate it etc. What they could say is dependent on how the ideas and information in the session were being heard and the way in which the test situation affords or constrains opportunities to make their own understanding clear. Importantly then, each teacher's understanding cannot be said to be personal to them since it depends on the situation in which it took place and on how others access it.

It is important to realise that all this is more than just saying that context matters. The argument is that knowledge simply cannot be separated from the situation in which it developed. Put simply, each of us needs others to be able to mean anything, since meaning is constituted *between* people. Though you can certainly sit by yourself and develop your thinking about something, this thinking still relies on the (cultural, social and historical) experiences you have had before. What is more, any attempt to share your 'new ideas' with others will require you to share also the historical and social/cultural basis on which you have developed them.

- In many senses, knowledge is distributed across all the people and artefacts involved in an event, not 'owned' by individuals.

- What I 'know' can be seen as a product of my history, the surrounding culture and the social setting in which I am 'knowing'.

Now, all this is rather philosophical and I will leave it to you, the reader, to make up your own mind about the extent to which you want to accept it. My own view is that it is quite a persuasive argument, but I would note that it does not stop me using other models of 'understanding' – which I can still view in personal, individual terms if I choose. What is important is not the truth of either way of thinking about understanding, but how perceiving things in different ways can help us to think differently about our classrooms. Putting aside the issue of its truth (or otherwise) therefore, let me offer some examples of its usefulness.

STOP AND THINK STOP

▶ For both of these classroom events consider how you might perceive them differently depending on your view of understanding as absolute and individual, or relative to time and place and distributed between people.

    1   A child says that she doesn't understand your explanation of how to add two 2-digit numbers using a number line.

    2   A child explains his solution for a problem to the class but it appears to make no sense.

In my own experience, viewing understanding as absolute and individual has often led me to view both of these common situations in terms of the child having a problem. In the first instance, the problem is a 'lack of understanding' on her part; in the second it is an 'inability to explain clearly'.

Sometimes this helps and I can 'solve' the child's problem for him/her, but viewing knowledge as relative and distributed casts the examples in a new light. In the first situation, if the understanding is *between* us then I need to look at my own explanation as much as at the child's comprehension and to ask: 'what is preventing us communicating successfully?'. In the second situation it is the other way around; I need to look at my ability to comprehend as much as at the child's ability to explain.

Have you ever noticed how other children in the class seem to be able to understand each other in ways that you cannot ('what she means is …')? These children are drawing on shared histories of working together and shared social and cultural experiences which are allowing them to 'understand' in ways not accessible to you and me.

What I hope is that my choice of words for the title of this chapter is now more apparent. 'Understanding mathematics through talk' would tend to imply individuality and completeness; by saying 'making mathematical meaning through talk' I hope that I have drawn your attention to both the incompleteness of understanding and the way in which understanding is 'made' ('constituted' is a better word perhaps) between people.

KEY IDEA

- Understanding can be seen as a corporate effort that is never finished.

I want now to consider *interacting through talk* as a vehicle for this meaning-making. You might remember though that I introduced the notion of *discourse* above, with the idea that talk was only one part of this. Two other parts are what we *do* and the nature of our social *expectations/norms*. Despite these two additions to the idea of discourse, I intend to focus on (mainly whole class) talk but to examine how our practices and expectations are intertwined with it.

Interacting through talk

Before launching into my own perspective on interaction through talk, I invite you to stop and think about your own theory in this respect. Again, I hope that, by doing so, you will subsequently be in a better position to make sense of (with?) what I have to say.

STOP AND THINK

▶ Imagine that you are asked to explain, by a visiting American teacher new to the PNS, why and how you work interactively with the whole class. Can you articulate a 'theory' justifying its use?

▶ How likely is your theory to lead to achieving the aims for maths teaching discussed in Chapter 2? Are the two in line with each other?

It is unlikely that you are able to simply articulate a theory about the use of whole class interaction, though, in trying, you may have begun to see what some of the issues are. We might consider at least the following.

- In the classroom, what is the role of the teacher? What about the pupils?

- How is the interaction between these people organised to allow it to take place most effectively?

- What kind of talk do you look for? Is there good talk and bad talk, or is all talk equally acceptable?

■ *What* are you hoping children will learn? Hopefully mathematical ideas, but, as was noted in Chapter 2, the nature of the experience affects the form of knowledge that children develop, as well as affecting their dispositions towards the subject.

Another, and perhaps the most challenging, issue is the question of actually *how* talk helps people to make sense of things. We are so used to talking that it is difficult to perceive what is going on when we do it. Neil Mercer, amongst many others, has explored this question and has pointed to the way in which language can be seen as a tool for thinking together – what he calls 'interthinking' (Mercer, 2000). He notes that this is more than simply 'communication', which, he says,

> *encourages the view of a linear process whereby people exchange ideas, think about them individually and then again exchange the products of their separate intellectual efforts. This does not do justice to the dynamic interaction of minds which language makes possible … 'interthinking' [refers to] the joint, co-ordinated intellectual activity which people regularly accomplish using language.*

> *(p. 16)*

As I talk with other people I am using words as (verbal) symbols for ideas, but I have no way of knowing for sure what those people mean by them. Fortunately, of course, our common cultural and linguistic upbringing means that our respective meanings are shared, at least sufficiently for the conversation to run smoothly. In everyday, casual conversation this is usually as far as things need go, but from time to time we need to make sense of new, more complex ideas with people and at such times we switch our talk into overdrive. Now some, perhaps many, ideas are not shared and so we engage in a process of making sense together through negotiation of the meaning behind the words. This is why, for example, given a 'simple' instruction, the recipients can still respond in different ways; why your insurance policy tries to define in advance terms such as 'the insured'; why different dictionaries give differing definitions of the same word; and how linguistic jokes work – for example, how you get two Whales in a mini (answer: up the motorway and over the Severn bridge!).

What language is *not*, is simply a way of transferring ideas from one individual to another. Crucially, it is the flexibility of the meaning of words that allows new sense to develop between people. If words were fixed and determined in advance, no such negotiation of meaning would be possible and ideas would become solidified and stuck.

It is because of the very *indeterminacy* of language, then, that people can make new meaning through talking (Mercer, 2000). Since one of the major purposes of schooling is to help pupils to do just this, the idea is particularly relevant to teaching. I hope that some implications are immediately obvious. I raise a few here to whet your appetite – though the point of subsequent chapters is to address them in more detail and see what they might mean in practice.

IN YOUR CLASSROOM

► Will your explanations automatically result in children understanding 'your' ideas? The way in which we help listeners to interact with explanations will be vital.

► How much time do you give for children to work out the meaning of potentially complex mathematical ideas? Children will need opportunities for extended speaking – with the teacher and/or with peers.

► How do you strike a balance between providing support for pupils talking about new ideas and dominating that conversation?

► Since working things out together may imply *not* agreeing to begin with, power relationships are important. Do your pupils feel free to use language to explore ideas and not be fearful of 'getting it wrong', or of contending other people's ideas – including yours?

Discourse and mathematics

You may remember that in the last chapter I briefly discussed the nature of maths as a discipline. Several points were particularly relevant:

■ Mathematics is the study of interrelated *ideas*, and is therefore fundamentally reliant on thinking.

■ These ideas can be abstracted from, and applied to, the physical world, but can also develop from other abstract ideas alone (you don't need the physical world to get from addition to multiplication, but it can help).

■ The subject is more than just a body of knowledge. It is also about dispositions, processes and procedures. You have to actually *do* mathematics.

Bearing these points in mind, what implications are there regarding the role of discourse in learning mathematics? Well, firstly, all classrooms have what we might call a *classroom discourse* – that is, a discourse associated with the business of being a pupil/teacher in a school setting. For example, ideas relating to groups, ability, objectives, the curriculum, assessment etc. will all be being made explicit or implicit through the ways in which the teachers and pupils interact with each other. Teachers and children share a common language for talking about these things. However, mathematics itself has its own discourse – there is a way to 'talk mathematics'. One implication for the classroom then is that we might want these two discourses to overlap as much as possible. Put simply, we want the children to talk mathematically because learning to *be* a mathematician is, in large part, the process of learning to talk like a mathematician.

As an analogy, think back to when you first began to teach. For student teachers, hearing experienced professionals talking in the staffroom can be daunting. For example, overhearing someone say that 'I've got a good set with some G & Ts but it's the level 3s that I need to push to improve the panda' may evoke strange zoological images for a student (is the panda ill perhaps after too much gin?), but run smoothly as part of the conversation between experienced staff. Even knowing the meaning of the words does not always help because it is not until we use them in a range of contexts that we become comfortable with their meaning.

The important point to understand here is that we are talking about more than just 'acquiring' mathematical *vocabulary*; though, of course, vocabulary will be important. Crucially, learning to use mathematical words neither precedes nor follows the understanding of the related idea. Rather, the two work hand in hand so that we come to understand the idea through trying to use the language associated with it. As I noted above, the indeterminacy of words and the need to negotiate meanings for them, allows, indeed drives, this process. Learning mathematics, then, is dependent on learning to speak the language of mathematics. And vocabulary is picked up *through* its use, not before its use, in a dynamic relationship between using words and understanding the associated ideas.

PRACTICAL EXAMPLE

Children in two parallel Year 3 classes are being introduced to the idea of 'diagonals' in 2D shapes. In the first class they are shown an oblong and told that the diagonal is the line that joins the two corners. They are then

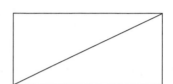

given some other shapes to draw diagonals on, but can only draw one diagonal for the hexagon, as shown by the solid line. When the teacher suggests other

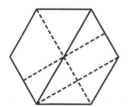

lines (dotted) they are not sure whether these are diagonals or not. One child complains that 'one is going the wrong way'. Superficially, they eventually agree with the teacher's new meaning of the term, but there is a sense that they don't really believe it!

In the class next door, the teacher plays a game with the children. She draws different shapes and marks a line on them that either is, or is not, a diagonal. For each one she asks: 'this is a diagonal: true or false?' and the children try to guess. As she then reveals the answer she puts the shapes in, or outside of, a ring marked with the label 'diagonals'. After several goes she asks the children to discuss in groups what they think a diagonal is. The debate that follows is heated, but after a few more shapes the class has agreed together on the conditions for a diagonal – straight, joining opposite corners, staying within the shape etc.

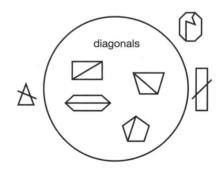

When the group is then asked about a hexagon they are still confused about some lines, but their earlier argument has prepared them to understand the word diagonal in a more flexible way and most children seem ready to accept this 'new' idea. One child notes that 'we need to add that to our definition'.

One thing to note about the example given above is that the agreement reached by the latter class is just that: an agreement. But this is true too of any definition, even ones in sophisticated mathematical dictionaries. One criticism that is sometimes levelled at me when I say this is that I am implying that any old definition will do and children are free to invent new meanings for everything. This is not the case. Though I'd never go as far as to say that one definition is 'right' above all others, good definitions will 'work' better – by which I mean they allow you to use them in new situations without breaking down. We saw this in the example above.

The key point though is that meaning cannot be 'given' to children. Instead, children have to constitute it – even if they do so only by having an internal conversation with themselves as they listen to the teacher. Of course we will need to tell children what words 'mean', but leaving it at that and not providing opportunities for them to play with the ideas and see the implications of the meaning will see them caught out when they have to put the words to use.

Pimm (1987) has a nice analogy in this respect. He suggests using the metaphor of learning a foreign language to illustrate this kind of approach to learning mathematics, namely that a foreign language can either be taught and *then* used or it can be taught *through* its use. Being taught a foreign language through its use implies the need for communication as the motivational driving force behind the development of the language. We learn to speak it because we need to communicate with people. The need to communicate about mathematics within a classroom might similarly drive the process of making sense. From this perspective, communication *leads* to knowing mathematical ideas; not vice versa where ideas might be 'learnt' first and then some how made use of.

IN YOUR CLASSROOM

▶ How often do you give children mathematics that they *need* to talk about (as opposed to you simply *wanting* them to talk about it)?

▶ When children come together for a plenary session are they all coming to talk about the same thing, or have different groups got different contributions to make? Which pattern is most likely to create a *need* to communicate about maths?

KEY IDEAS 💡

■ We need to try to create classroom tasks in which communication about maths is *part* of the task, not incidental to it.

■ Ideally, children (and their teachers) should begin to see understanding as something that is never completed and as shared between people (we understand more together when we communicate about it).

Quality versus quantity

In the paragraphs above I have tried to demonstrate the need for a mathematical discourse taking place in the classroom. Rather than being supplementary to the learning of mathematics, I am saying that it is fundamental to it; you cannot learn mathematics (indeed any subject) in any depth without developing the discourse associated with it. Discourse and understanding go hand-in-hand.

What, then, is the nature of this discourse? Will any discourse do, or are we looking for particular forms? And is more talk necessarily better? In short, the answer to these questions is that quality, not quantity, is what matters. What we need is high quality discourse – and then plenty of it. Unfortunately, research is clearly showing (e.g. Alexander, 2000) that in the UK we tend to adopt teaching approaches in which the discourse is highly unstructured. Generally, children do a lot of informal talking but are not necessarily expected to make themselves understood. Verbal language is certainly not as highly valued, nor expected to be as accurate, as written language. This lack of quality is not made up for by the high quantity in comparison to other countries where, importantly, though more formal in style, the rationale for classroom discourse is clear to both teachers and pupils. In these other contexts, children and teachers are clear that communicating in forms other than writing – verbal and non-verbal – is not simply a social affair. Rather, it is the vehicle through which understanding can be developed. It is, if you like, 'the work' being done.

PRACTICAL EXAMPLE

Carlos, a Year 6 child, is asked by his teacher how he is trying to calculate 24 $\times$ 34. The dialogue runs as follows:

C: *I did … I knew ten 3s were … [pauses]*

T: *Ten 3s are 30, yes? … but are they 3s?*

C: *Er … 10? … 30?…*

T: *[Interrupting] That's right, they are 30s. Well 34 really. So ten 34s are 340. OK? Good, so go on …*

C: *Then I did … I did, no … I did double…*

T: *[Interrupting] 20 is twice 10, isn't it?*

C: *Yeh …*

T: *So that's what?*

C: *680?*

T: *Good. And then what about the four 34s?*

C: *Two 34s are … [calculates in his head] … 68.*

T: *Good. So double again and you get …*

C: *… 120 …*

T: *[Interrupting] … 30. 130. In fact it's 136, isn't it? Well done Carlos.*

▶ Look back at the dialogue. What has Carlos actually said?

▶ What expectations do you have of children as they talk about their mathematics in your classroom?

In the example above, you might have felt that the problem was that the teacher dominated the conversation and did not let Carlos say what he wanted. Without being there it is hard to know. Another interpretation is that perhaps Carlos chose to be led by the teacher. The point is that discourse in general, and verbal exchanges in particular, are about more than just making sense of ideas. People use language (and other aspects of the discourse, such as body posture) to 'position' themselves socially. So, the teacher 'puts herself in charge' through her comments and responses, children retire into the background by non-response, others push themselves forward by answering with authority and so on.

Now, clearly this is a very complex area, impossible to analyse in depth for every case. Nevertheless, one point seems common to all situations: people will tend to align themselves with an authoritative voice; with whom they perceive as expert. This is, of course, a good thing if we want children to adopt the view of one other person, but if our goal is to encourage children to inter-think (as Mercer, 2000 calls it) then we need to watch carefully for dominant voices.

What we are trying to achieve then, in order to create effective discourse for thinking mathematically, is a situation in which children are involved in a genuine attempt to make sense of ideas together and where they learn, gradually, to bring their own ideas and opinions to a discussion and to reason about them. Against this, we have to balance the need for the teacher to maintain order and fulfil the expectations that the curriculum imposes on him or her. This, needless to say, is no mean task. In the next chapter, we begin to take up the challenge.

Summary

- *Understanding* is more problematic than we often consider it to be. It can be seen as relative to time and context and can be thought of as distributed between people.

▶ How might viewing it this way change some of the things we do, and the ways we think, as teacher?

- *Discourse* is about what is said, but also what is done and what is expected. In terms of language, ideas in the form of words are constantly being negotiated between people. It is this that allows new ideas to emerge.

▶ What might be the dangers, in terms of teaching, of assuming that words simply 'carry' meaning?

- Mathematics teaching should allow time for children to talk about their ideas. Like language learning, although there will be a time for learning the 'vocabulary' of new procedures, the need to communicate can be the driving force for getting children thinking mathematically.

- We want mathematical discourse in our classrooms to be high quality. Creating tasks for children to talk about and demanding that they take care over spoken language can help us to do this.

► How do children talk in your class? What expectations are there on them – and on you?

📖 Further reading

Mercer, N. (2000) *Words and Minds*. London: Routledge.
Pratt, N. (2002) 'Mathematics *As* Thinking', *Mathematics Teaching*, 181, 34–7.

CHAPTER 4

The challenges of whole class interaction

This chapter will ...

- develop the idea of *discourse*, introduced in Chapter 3, in relation to the whole class setting;

- make the distinction between *classroom discourse* and *mathematical discourse* and consider how these are often in tension with each other;

- look carefully at what tends to happen in whole class teaching from both teachers' and children's perspectives. This prepares the way to consider how to maximise the mathematical discourse.

What is good interactive teaching?

In the previous chapter I introduced the idea of *discourse* to describe the *talk* (what is said), *practices* (what is done) and *expectations* (what is expected/meant) in any social situation. If you have followed the discussion you may be feeling confident that the kinds of pedagogical approaches adopted by schools in the early part of the twenty-first century must have had a major impact on teachers in this respect. After all, whole class interactive teaching, including the use of a discursive plenary in which the class is meant to talk together about the learning that has taken place in the lesson, has a far higher profile now than in the past. Government guidance instructs teachers that

> *High quality direct teaching is oral, interactive and lively ... It is a two-way process in which pupils are expected to play an active part by answering questions, contributing points to discussions, and explaining and demonstrating their methods to the class.*

> *(DfEE, 1999a, p. 1:11)*

Other official documents similarly note that 'effective interaction'

maximises the opportunity for the teacher to interact with the pupils, so that they can talk and be listened to, and receive feedback that helps them to develop their mathematical knowledge, skills and understanding; and

allows pupils to show what they know, explain their thinking and methods and suggest alternative ways of tackling problems.

(DfEE, 1998, p. 14)

STOP AND THINK

> ► Try reinterpreting the statements above in terms of *discourse*.

> ► What are the statements saying about how the discourse in the classroom should look?

In my view, the statements can be interpreted as saying that good mathematics teaching takes place when there is a high level of mathematical discourse in the classroom. In other words, they highlight the importance of encouraging children to learn maths by articulating their own mathematical thinking. Children need to:

- talk about their maths;
- show their thinking visually;
- respond to other people's ideas;
- adapt their thinking in the light of suggestions;
- ask and respond to questions;
- carry out mathematical tasks;
- behave in mathematical ways.

Meanwhile, teachers need to:

- initiate talk;
- facilitate discussions;
- listen carefully to children;
- ask and respond to questions;
- provide tasks to complete and to talk about;
- understand the subject well enough to model acting mathematically;
- have certain mathematical expectations of children, and evaluate these.

So are these instructions borne out in practice? Though individual cases differ, the overall picture seems to be that, far from improving the mathematical discourse, the NNS (and the NLS) have actually reduced it. Increasingly, studies are showing that:

whole class talk is being used by the teacher for 'teaching' rather than being an instrument for learning. The emphasis on transmission of information and factual questions reflects the concern with content and the awareness of the need to meet objectives.

(Burns and Myhill, 2004, p. 47)

Discourses of interactive teaching

So why are changes to teaching approaches which have been designed to increase the amount of mathematical discussion in the classroom actually having the opposite effect in many classrooms?

The idea of discourse can help us to unpick this conundrum. The key point is that in any situation there are usually several discourses involved at once. Classrooms are no exception – there is, at least:

- the *classroom discourse*; and

- the discourse of the *mathematics* itself.

Remember, these 'discourses' are only ideas; ways of considering the situation. Discourses are not there waiting to be touched. But thinking this way helps us to realise that in a classroom the teacher is trying to achieve two jobs at once.

KEY IDEAS

- The teacher's job requires her to manage the classroom so that it runs 'as it should'. This demands that she works within a *classroom discourse* (involving objectives, groups, targets, behaviour etc.).

- At the same time she is trying to develop a *mathematical discourse* with the children (involving thinking and acting mathematically).

- These two discourses are often not easy to combine effectively, but the way in which they are managed strongly affects the quality of learning. Ideally, the classroom discourse should support the mathematical one so that children can focus on the latter.

Managing the way in which the classroom and mathematical discourses overlap, or interfere with each other, is the key to successful interactive maths teaching.

In the following extract Frances, a Year 5/6 teacher, describes how she feels about her maths teaching.

▶ Try to identify references to the mathematical and classroom discourses in what she says.

'I think it is difficult. Firstly, there's the external pressure, that we are supposed to cover so many objectives and if you don't, how are they going to get on [in Year 6] … oh we haven't done this and we haven't done this. So from that point of view I feel that the school is under pressure to get children to a certain level. So you don't want to be knocked off your path because otherwise you can't tick it off your list; whether they've got it or not. The other thing, I think, is issues of classroom management. Sometimes if you go off down one particular path then, if the other children, if they're not interested, then it can cause problems in terms of keeping them all focused. I think it's a shame because you need to be a bit spontaneous and give them a chance to discover that they're wrong. You want to get them thinking about the maths, trying to see ideas and connections. Then you can get them on board and hopefully work towards your objective. And in terms of putting the onus for talking about maths back on the children, I think I do do that … I am a bit more flexible in that respect. But in terms of these objectives that we are supposed to cover and get children to at different stages, yes I do feel that sometimes – "oh no, no, we can't go off down that way".'

▶ To what extent do you identify with Frances' point of view?

If we now go back to the quotation above from Burns and Myhill (2004), we can see the tension that Frances describes so clearly. That 'whole class teaching is being used by the teacher for *teaching* rather than being an instrument for learning' simply points to the emphasis on classroom discourse at the expense of the mathematical discourse. In other words, they are suggesting that we can tend to become so focused on making the class operate in particular ways that we actually prevent children from engaging mathematically in any depth.

This brings us back to the idea of *intent* introduced in Chapter 3. For whilst we may act 'by the book' in terms of our interactive teaching, our intent often appears to be too focused on the discourse of the classroom, not the mathematics. But before looking at how we might redress this balance, we need to analyse what goes on in whole class interactive teaching in greater depth.

What interactive teaching might look like

Interactive teaching is obviously highly complex but it is possible to describe certain features that it might include. Table 4.1 lays out some of these features, all taken from guidance that teachers have been offered by government initiatives. Unfortunately, whilst such guidance has been plentiful in terms of *what* to do, less has been said about the reason for doing it. The second column, therefore, shows my interpretation of what the intent could be for each feature; the way it can affect positively the mathematical discourse in the group. My perspective is in no way comprehensive and you might like to add your own ideas – or challenge mine!

Table 4.1 Features of interactive teaching

Features of interactive teaching	*Positive effects on mathematical discourse*
Asking questions of the class or individuals	■ Prompts and facilitates mathematical talk ■ Opens up new areas for children to think about ■ Encourages children to reason about their mathematics ■ Requires children to communicate their thinking to others ■ Generates a rough indication of current thinking
Demonstrating or modelling mathematical ideas	■ Provides an insight into how to carry out mathematical procedures ■ Provides a visual explanation of a mathematical idea ■ Models ways of 'acting mathematically' ■ Models the meaning of 'process' words (e.g. reasoning, estimate etc.) ■ Models mathematical thinking and behaviour
Evaluating and correcting children's responses	■ Helps children to understand what is mathematically sound, and what is not ■ Models mathematical expectations

One noticeable feature of this list of government recommendations is that, despite the claim that interactive teaching is 'a two-way process' in which children can 'talk and be listened to', all the directions appear to be about talking *to* (possibly at!) children – reflecting Burns and Myhill's observation. I would therefore add two more points to the table, as follows.

Table 4.2 Additional features of interactive teaching

Facilitating discussion between pupils	■ Helps children to learn to communicate with each other ■ Encourages children to evaluate each other's responses ■ Models mathematical discourse
Listening carefully to children's mathematical responses	■ Models active, respectful listening ■ Values children's ideas ■ Improves assessment opportunities

What happens in practice?

Tables 4.1 and 4.2 show my attempt to describe what effective interactive teaching with a whole class might involve. It is crucial to understand that although the elements in the left hand column may describe the practices involved, it is the intentions in the right hand column that are vital; making it more likely that the learning is effective. My feeling is that advice to teachers over the last ten years has lost sight of this point and has encouraged us to think that simply *acting* in a particular way will generate effective learning. My message is simple, and runs contrary to this: do not worry so much about what you *do*; worry more about what you *mean*.

Though this message appears straightforward, it is not to say that it is easy in practice. We cannot ignore classroom discourse; after all, we are working in a classroom and our number one priority is that the class runs smoothly enough to be effective … and to be acceptable to those around us, not to mention preserving our own sanity. It is inevitable that the need to satisfy different demands on us will lead to tensions. However, what we can do is become more aware of these tensions and what might be happening when we act in certain ways.

To begin to investigate this, I have brought together the sections of the tables above and considered them again in terms of some of the tensions that might arise for teachers. Note that interactive teaching is, as we have noted, inherently filled with tensions, like a juggling act in which many different plates need to be kept spinning at once. You cannot get rid of such tensions; they are part and parcel of teaching. You can learn to work with them more effectively though and the first step to doing so is to understand them well.

a) Asking questions of the class or of individuals

IN YOUR CLASSROOM

Are your questions aimed at:

▶ encouraging extended mathematical talk between pupils, or …

▶ checking up on what children are thinking?

If trying to encourage talk, are you:

▶ helping children make sense of an idea together as a group, or …

▶ trying to engineer the 'right' response so that you can pick up on it?

If checking what children are thinking, are you:

▶ encouraging other children to interact with what is said, or …

▶ expecting other children to listen to, and remember, it?

Note how each pair of prompts in the box offers the chance for the lesson to either diverge (the first prompt each time) or converge (the second). We are constantly juggling the freedom for children to talk about their ideas with the need to keep these 'on track' in terms of the theme (objective) that we want to cover – remember Frances' comments in the interview above. But each time we focus too heavily on managing the discussion the tendency is for the focus to switch from the mathematical discourse to the classroom discourse; children stop thinking mathematically and start thinking about the strategies involved in being a successful pupil – doing what you want them to do.

PRACTICAL EXAMPLE

Felix is working on the properties of two dimensional shape with his Year 4 group who all have a set of plastic shapes on the table in front of them. The following dialogue takes place:

F: *Hold up a regular pentagon. How many lines of symmetry does it have?*

Ch1:   *One.*

F: *One? Why do you think that?*

Ch1:   *Because the only way you can fold it is straight down the middle [the child indicates a line vertically down the centre].*

F: *Ok. What do other people think?*

Ch2:   *Five [the correct answer].*

F: *Five, ok. Now hold up regular hexagons. How many lines of symmetry do they have? …*

Note how Felix's first question, and the task (to find the regular pentagon), imply that the children are about to be involved in a discussion about the properties of shape. But in fact, this is not what transpires. By asking for other children's ideas when the wrong answer is given, but moving on immediately when the right answer appears, the intent behind his actions seems more to do with hearing correct responses.

▶ How might this have felt different if Felix had asked again what other people thought in response to child 2, *without* revealing whether five was right or wrong?

Though, alone, this example may seem unimportant, repeatedly getting into this kind of pattern, with the spotlight on the accuracy of the answer and the emphasis on 'checking up', persuades children that you do not really want them to engage in thinking about the maths … and of course they will obligingly stop doing so!

b) Demonstrating or modelling mathematical ideas

Do you model or demonstrate:

▶ to show children what *might* be done, or …

▶ to tell children what *must* be done?

In modelling/demonstrating are you:

▶ focusing on the process, making the mathematical discourse explicit by talking out loud about what you are thinking and doing, or …

▶ focusing on the outcome, telling children what the end result should be/look like?

During your modelling/demonstrating:

▶ do you invite comment from children, perhaps by pausing from time to time and asking 'what next, do you think?', or …

▶ do you expect children to watch quietly in order to remember what is being done?

Notice, this time, how the focus of the first point in each pair is on engaging the children in the mathematical elements of what is being done – the mathematical discourse. Maintaining an air of uncertainty and conjecture, focusing on process not product and inviting comment all help to keep the spotlight on the process of *doing* maths. This contrasts with the second point in each pair which focuses on outcomes. There is nothing wrong with focusing on outcomes from time to time, indeed this may well be a useful thing to do. However, done repeatedly, it encourages children to think of the subject as a set of ideas to remember/acquire, not as a process of enquiry.

Margarita is working on counting with her reception class, all of whom have been given a mini whiteboard and pen. She makes clear that she wants them to watch, then draws a dot on the board and counts 'one'. Then she draws two more dots underneath to form a triangle and counts 'one, two'. She then pauses and asks children what they think comes next, encouraging them to 'draw it and talk to a partner'. Margarita draws the three dots in the next row and counts 'one, two, three'. She doesn't stop to ask what the children drew – anyone who didn't get it sees her model the correct answer anyway. Now, without needing to say anything she points to the space below the line of three and shrugs her shoulders, inviting ideas from the children about what is on the next line. This continues with children counting higher until she breaks her silence, changing the task by asking 'how many are in the whole triangle I wonder?'. She then models counting them all.

c) Evaluating and correcting children's responses

Do you view inaccurate answers as:

▶ opportunities to explore how the class is thinking about a topic, or ...

▶ as mistakes, to be put right?

Do you arrive at the accurate answer:

▶ by allowing children to argue for their own answer until its inaccuracy becomes apparent, or ...

▶ by making clear what is accurate and what is inaccurate and expecting children to remember the accurate one?

It is very easy when under pressure managing a class of children to revert to what is right and what is wrong. In particular, if our focus is on objectives as the end-points of lessons, we can easily drive children towards the acquisition of particular information rather than allowing them to use language to develop fuller understandings together. Treating *all* answers as examples of mathematical thinking, but of varying accuracy, places the emphasis again on the mathematical discourse, since the task becomes to ascertain whether or not the thinking holds water mathematically. This differs subtly, but significantly, from talking about right and wrong, which tends to focus again on the classroom discourse of 'success', 'achievement' and 'ability'.

The practical example on the facing page shows how this might work in practice.

What I like about the following lesson extract is the way in which the accurate answer is made clear to everyone, but how Amy and Gita come to see this for themselves. Not only does this diminish the impact of 'being wrong', but the whole event models nicely the 'business' of mathematics. In a tiny way, these children are doing what professional mathematicians do: publishing their ideas, laying them open to scrutiny and repairing the flaws that others find in them. It is mathematical creativity in action.

In the following example, Nigel interacts with a class of Year 3 children who are trying to calculate 7 $\times$ 13 as part of a larger problem they are tackling together.

▶ How does he keep the emphasis on mathematical thinking and still ascertain what is accurate?

Amy: 80 [inaccurate]

N: [writes 80 on the board without giving away the (in)accuracy of the answer] Anyone get a different answer?

Taro: 91 [accurate]

N: [again, writes 91, not revealing the accuracy] Any more answers?

Gita: 90 [records 90, as before]

N: Ok, we've got 80, 91 and 90. Who can argue for their answer?

Amy: I can. Seven 10s are 70 and 7 add 3 is ...

Luke: [interrupting] No. It's not 7 add 3, it's seven 3s. 21.

N: [to Amy] Can you argue back? What do you think?

Amy: [thinks] ... No ... 91.

N: [to Gita] What do you think now?

Gita: Yes, 91.

N: Ok, 91. Looks like we all agree. What other mistakes might we make with this one?

Noel: We might do 7 add 13. 20.

And the conversation continues briefly to look at this.

d) Facilitating discussion between pupils; listening carefully to their responses

Does the conversation:

▶ flow between pupils and yourself, or ...

▶ bounce back and forth between you and individual children?

With children's responses do you:

▶ consider seriously what they imply about mathematical thinking and follow this up, or ...

▶ appropriate them for your teaching so that you can stick within your agenda?

What is your talking : listening ratio:

▶ 30:70 ... 50:50, or ...

▶ 60:40 ... 90:10?

Studies into how interaction takes place with groups of children have long shown that teachers tend to get into what is often called an 'Initiation–Response–Feedback', or IRF, pattern. The teacher will ask a question (initiation), gain a response from the child and then evaluate that response themselves (feedback).

PRACTICAL EXAMPLE

Look at the following snippet from an interaction with a Year 2/3 class.

▶ Can you see the IRF pattern?

Teacher: How did you calculate 43 plus 27?

Child 1:   I did 3 and 7 is 10 and then 4 and 2 is 6 and that made 70.

Teacher: Ok, good. So you did the ones first and then the tens.

Did anyone do it another way?

Child 2:   I did 40 and 20 and added the 3 and the 7.

Teacher: Very good. So you did the tens first, well done.

Note how the teacher evaluates the children's responses both in terms of value ('good', 'well done') and what was done ('so you did …'). I stress that there is nothing wrong with this IRF pattern in itself and teachers use it effectively on a regular basis. Again though, it is a matter of intent. Used all the time it becomes habitual and sends out the message 'I will ask the questions and I will be the judge of the response'. You might be able to see that this tends to focus us again on the *classroom* discourse – the rules of engagement, if you like. More importantly, perhaps, it also implies 'I will do the thinking for you'. This disempowers children from engaging in the *mathematical* discourse and tends to discourage them from perceiving the subject as a creative, decision-making process. Instead, the message that maths is about a body of knowledge owned by the teacher and to be acquired by the learner is reinforced.

In place of this IRF pattern we might want a pattern that allows, indeed encourages, children to become involved in the evaluation phase as well as the response phase. If we are more ambitious, we might even aim to have them involved in asking the questions in the first place too. One thing of interest is that government guidance has focused a lot on the questions we ask. For example, the vocabulary book published as part of the National Numeracy Strategy has a useful section at the start that lists different kinds of mathematical questions (DfEE, 1999c, pp. 4–6). But what the IRF pattern points to is that it is your *response* to the child that matters just as much. Far less attention has been paid to this – perhaps because it is more complex in that you cannot plan it in advance. In the next chapter we will consider responding in detail, but for now consider how each of the following phrases might have been used in the response phase by the teacher in the example above – and what difference this might have made.

- 'Interesting. What do people think of that?'

- 'OK. Any thoughts?'

- 'Can you tell us more?'

Appropriating children's ideas for teaching

As well as simply falling into the IRF mould, which affects the *pattern* of the discourse, teachers often *appropriate* children's responses in order to control the *direction* of the thinking that they want to take place (remember Burns and Myhill's quote about using interaction for teaching, not for learning, at the start of this chapter).

PRACTICAL EXAMPLE

In the following exchange Gordon is asking his Year 4 class how they divided 484 by 4. The lesson objective is the use of 'chunking' – repeatedly taking away multiples of 4 until zero is reached.

G: *So what did you do?*

Child 1:   *I knew that 48 divided by 4 was …*

G: *[interrupting] … but how did you do it, by chunking?*

Child 2:   *I took away 80 because …*

G: *Good. 80 is 20 lots of 4, isn't it. So then what? You were left with … what?*

Child 2:   *I knew that 404 was 101 lots …*

G: *[interrupting] … ok, so you said that 484 less 80 was 404. Then, 400 is four 100s and then four more. Then what could we have done?*

Child 2:   *Then it would have been 101 fours.*

Gordon: *Yes, great. So it's what in the end … It's 100 and 1 and 20 fours, isn't it.*

Child 2:   *121*

Gordon: *Yes. Good.*

Note how Gordon controls the 'discussion' by interrupting the children and using the answers to illustrate his teaching point – even though the children appear to be able to solve the problem their own way. The end result is that the 'explanation' belongs more to Gordon than to the children.

IN YOUR CLASSROOM

▶ Which of these forms of appropriation can you catch yourself using?

▶ Why are you doing each one and how is it useful, or not, in your teaching?

- *Interrupting* answers to questions and/or finishing them off in your own words.

- *Reinterpreting* what had been said to mean something different.

- *Ignoring* the whole answer because it didn't match the teaching point.

- *Ignoring* the whole answer for fear that it could not be understood.

- *Ignoring* elements of the answer in order to refocus it on something new.

- *Repeating* the answer, but emphasising certain parts of it to change the meaning.

- Using *selective hearing* to deliberately ignore unwanted responses.

- Using *value judgements* ('good', 'I'm not sure about that', quizzical looks etc.) to endow certain aspects of the answer with special significance.

Once again, of course, using these forms of appropriation is necessary and quite appropriate much of the time; after all, we can't just let the discussion meander aimlessly wherever it wants to go. Focusing children on particular points is often an effective way to support their thinking too.

If it becomes habitual and constant though, children soon learn that you are not genuinely interested in their responses, except in as far as they serve your (teaching) purpose. Appropriating responses can then become inappropriate – what we might call inappropriation! The focus then returns to the classroom discourse; this time in terms of the 'game' of providing the teacher with the answers she or he wants to avoid disharmony and keep the lesson 'on track'. As a result, children tend to switch off their mathematical thinking and drift into a kind of default, line-of-least-resistance behaviour. The trick is to manage to steer the conversation enough to maintain its flow, but without getting the children to switch off in this way.

KEY IDEAS

- Teachers' interactions with children involve a balance between the ongoing mathematical and classroom discourses.

- This balance is affected by many things, including the ways in which teachers:

  - ask questions;

  - respond to and appropriate children's ideas;

  - model and demonstrate;

  - evaluate and correct responses;

  - facilitate discussion and listen carefully.

- The most effective interaction is likely to happen when children's focus is more explicitly on the mathematical discourse with the classroom discourse being implicit and in the background.

Children's perspectives on interactive teaching

In this chapter so far I have been focusing on interaction from the adult's point of view. In doing so I have suggested a number of things that might affect the way children perceive the classroom discourse involved in the whole class interactive parts of their lessons. Are these borne out in practice though? What do children really think is going on?

Though it is impossible to respond to these questions for all children in all classrooms, my own observations in this area point to a number of answers. In one project, children from Years 2 and 6 were asked to look at video excerpts from their own lessons taught by their usual class teachers and to recount what they thought was going on. Their ideas illustrated a number of key points about the classroom discourse – how learning was taking place and how it felt to them.

STOP AND THINK

▶ If children in your class watched a video of their lessons with you, what might they say was happening?

▶ What would they say about *how* learning takes place through this form of interaction?

In my own study – and bearing in mind that all three of the teachers involved were, from a subjective point of view, doing a good job – children understood the general idea of class interaction for making meaning jointly together. In terms of *what* was being learnt, encouragingly children seemed to realise that the whole idea was to work together on ideas.

On the other hand they tended to think of this as 'making the right idea public and then remembering it'. The focus was on what they should end up with 'in their minds', rather than on the process of constructing a new idea together – reflecting an individual and absolute view of understanding, as outlined in the last chapter.

In terms of *how* this learning took place, children pointed to three important ideas.

1 'Teacher is judge and jury'

Children perceived the teacher as the ultimate arbiter of right and wrong, reinforcing my conjecture above that teachers tend to use value judgements to appropriate children's thinking and mark out what is to be considered correct.

Though not a bad thing per se, we noted that this can lead to impoverished interaction if it becomes a game of 'provide the right answer'. It can also suggest to children that they do not need to do the thinking themselves because if they wait long enough the teacher will do it for them and tell them what to think.

2 'Listening matters; talking doesn't'

Though the children all tended to say that listening and talking were both important, there was a subtle difference in terms of the value of each one. Whilst listening was seen as a *means of learning* ('we learn by hearing what others say'), talking was not. In fact, from the children's point of view, the value of talking was only in as far as it gave us something to listen to – what one might call 'listening fodder'. This was linked to the idea that, whatever the purpose of working together was, what really mattered was remembering what the teacher signalled as the 'right' thing.

Now, of course, children are bound to point to the value of listening, if only because they do far more of it than talking! But if they do not see talking as a *way of making sense of things* they are unlikely to value it greatly – and unlikely to engage in it seriously and carefully. Ideally, we want children to see talking as an important part of their mathematical 'work'.

IN YOUR CLASSROOM

▶ Do children pay attention to how they speak and see it as part of learning?

▶ Do you?

▶ How could you improve children's attention to their speaking and make them see it as part of their 'work'?

Incidentally, even though listening was important in children's minds, for many of them it seemed to be a kind of waiting game. Like coarse fishermen (and women), children appeared to be waiting on the river bank for the 'right thing' to come along – a linguistic pike, perhaps – in order to catch it for consumption (remembering). This compared sharply with a few children whose listening was more active. These were the fly fishers who regularly waded proactively into the water themselves to find the most interesting pools and who played the fish with a range of verbal flies to see which generated the most interesting results!

3 'We can't follow the discussion'

Children pointed out that the way interaction took place in the classroom often prevented them from taking part effectively. Amongst other things they noted that:

■ There were *expert explainers* in the class to whom it was worth listening, but …

■ … there were also other children whose explanations never made sense, causing them to switch off immediately.

■ Explanations were always directed at the teacher, often making it hard to hear them, especially for those sitting behind the speaker. Volume, seating position and lack of clarity all meant that they often could not hear properly.

■ Explanations were boring to listen to if you already knew the answer … 'why should we listen?'

► Which children are the 'expert' explainers ... which are the 'novices'?

► If you were not in front of the child, being spoken *to*, could you hear the explanation well?

► Do the other children *need* to hear this explanation? Is it adding something new to the discussion?

Children, unsurprisingly, have a strong sense of what is going on in the classroom and we might do well to ask them more about it. At the very least, the points made above may provide some starting points for considering what happens in your own classroom.

Summary

■ Both mathematical and classroom discourses are going on hand-in-hand in teaching. We want the weighting to be towards the former – bearing in mind that we have to live with(in) the latter.

► How has reading this chapter helped you to see your classroom differently in these terms? What insights has this distinction given you, if any?

■ There are a number of features that effective interactive teaching is likely to have, but the key issue is the intent behind each one, not the act itself.

► Have you developed a new awareness of the *effect* of aspects of your interactive teaching – demonstrating, questioning, responding etc?

■ Teachers *appropriate* children's responses for their own (teaching) ends. This is both a good thing and a bad thing.

► What forms of appropriation are you aware of in your own practice, and what effect do they have on the children's thinking about, and feeling towards, the subject?

■ Children themselves understand the classroom discourse very well and may have a lot to tell us about how to change it so that there can be a greater emphasis on the mathematics.

► What might children say about your classroom and the way that it (and you) operates?

📖 Further reading

Alexander, R. (2004) *Towards Dialogic Teaching: Rethinking Classroom Talk*. York: Dialogos.
DfES/QCA (2003) *Speaking, Listening, Learning: Working With Children in Key Stages 1 and 2*. London: DfES Publications. (Also downloadable from www.standards.dfes.gov.uk).

CHAPTER 5

Thinking, talking and acting mathematically

> This chapter will …
>
> ■ briefly review the challenges of whole class interactive teaching, outlined in the previous chapter;
>
> ■ discuss the central importance of creating a *need to communicate* in order to maximise the focus on the mathematical discourse in the classroom;
>
> ■ present ways to begin to tackle the challenges, with examples of how they might work in practice.

Reviewing the challenges of whole class interaction

In Chapter 4 I presented a number of challenges for teachers in teaching the whole class interactively. Central to these challenges was the notion that classrooms are social settings – albeit particular ones – and therefore run on social lines, and according to particular norms and expectations. In particular they have their own discourse – the discourse of schooling. Though we want children to engage in 'doing' mathematics, thinking mathematically and coming to understand it through interaction with resources and with each other, the discourse of schooling frequently interferes with this in practice. Children focus on what makes them successful, which is often more about classroom behaviour (in the broadest sense) than about mathematical behaviour. The challenge for teachers is that they must juggle these two competing discourses.

In the following table these issues are summarised again, with the challenge for teachers made clear for each one. The first column notes the issue; the second points to the potential problem in relation to the focus on the classroom discourse; the third poses the challenge as a question for us, asking how we might refocus on the mathematical discourse.

Table 5.1 Challenges of whole class interaction

Issue	Potential Problem (focus on classroom discourse)	Challenge (focus on mathematical discourse)
Questioning	Questions too often may be evaluative, focusing children on right/wrong, good/bad, able/unable, rather than on seeing mathematics as the business of thinking about problems.	How can we refocus our questioning so that we encourage children to think more about their mathematics, whilst still retaining a sense of direction in our teaching?
Responding to questions – evaluating children's ideas	Evaluating children's responses often leads to judgements that reinforce the right/wrong issue above. This encourages children to think of maths as 'acquiring the right answer' not as thinking mathematically.	How can we show children that all answers are examples of mathematical thinking, but of varying accuracy? How can we encourage them to see mathematics as being about exploring the accuracy of this thinking?
Being judge and jury	Though we will need to judge children's responses, continually setting ourselves up as judge and jury also encourages an 'acquisition' model and relieves them of having to take responsibility for thinking.	How can we evaluate children's thinking effectively but without taking over to the extent that they must think what we think ... or not think at all?
Facilitating discussion between pupils	What is called 'discussion' is often an Initiation-Response-Feedback (IRF) pattern – more interrogation than discussion. This can force children to play find-the-right-answer and lead them down a path of 'least resistance'. It also privileges the most able.	How can we develop our discussions so that all children are encouraged to think mathematically and at some depth? How can we change our responses to stop discussions bouncing back and forth between teacher and child?
Modelling and demonstrating	Modelling and demonstrating can become a lesson in what *must* be done rather than a chance to think about what might be done. Again, this focuses children on products, not processes.	How can we maintain the value of seeing how to do something, but encourage children to critique it and see its relevance to them?
Inappropriately using children's thinking (what I called '[in]appropriating').	We need to focus and drive group thinking and not let it wander aimlessly, but we can tend to take over children's ideas, convincing them that our own agenda is what really matters. This discourages them from thinking for themselves.	How can we make effective use of what children say without controlling their thinking too much? How can we avoid 'inappropriation', with discussions becoming a game of 'providing the right answers'?
Viewing listening as more important for learning than talking	Talking can be seen only as 'listening fodder' and not as an important learning activity in its own right. This can lead to listening and talking becoming a 'duty' for children rather than being part of their mathematical 'work'.	How can we encourage children to see talking as an important part of their mathematical work? How can we develop their ability to talk effectively for this purpose?
Not being able to follow the discussion	Children themselves report the difficulty of being involved in class discussions – for practical and educational reasons.	How can we facilitate better communication between pupils? How can we make whole class interaction enjoyable and purposeful so that they want to engage in it?

Separating out these issues as I have done in the table above helps, I hope, in understanding them and in seeing what the challenges for us are. Unfortunately, when it comes to considering what we might do about them this delineation is not so helpful because the issues are so interlinked. For example, asking questions and responding to answers are usefully considered together; and being judge and jury might be involved in most of the other issues. More importantly, what I hope I have managed to make clear in this book so far is that it is not enough to consider only what to 'do'. We need instead to consider how this will be understood by children – what the intent is seen to be. This is the aspect of whole class teaching that I think has been ignored by much of the government advice over the years.

Instead of taking each issue separately, then, I want to begin to unpick some answers by considering principles that should underpin our whole class teaching, before bringing these to life through examples in practice. These principles are drawn together under three headings:

- Creating purposeful mathematical activity

- Asking and responding to questions

- Encouraging children to talk clearly and accurately

In the two chapters that follow I then provide some starting points for lessons that are proactive in initiating effective whole class interaction, focusing on number and on shape and space in each chapter respectively.

Creating purposeful mathematical activity

At the risk of stating the obvious, children are unlikely to engage in mathematical work that is not purposeful and for which they cannot see a point. Though this statement may *appear* to be obvious, its subtlety is in the nature of the 'point' that children see.

Ainley et al. (2006) note that a good task has a 'purpose' for children; not in the sense of being somehow useful outside the classroom (though it may be), but in the sense that the outcome is meaningful to them in terms of its product. This still leaves open the issue of the kind of meaning it holds though. In Chapter 2 I argued that it is vital for teachers to understand something of what the subject is about because the way in which children experience mathematics affects not how much knowledge they 'acquire', but the kind of knowledge they develop. Children taught through problem solving and mathematical thinking simply develop a different kind of mathematical knowledge than those taught through explanation and routine practice.

The kind of purposeful meaning I am looking for in tasks is that in which children have a definite product to create (mental/virtual or physical); a goal to achieve. If the children are asked after the event what they did in maths today I want them to say 'we created a poster' or 'we created a way to find prime numbers', not just 'we did subtraction'. The lack of such products is, I believe, one of the negative things about recent curriculum reforms. These reforms have promoted the idea of focusing on the teaching (adult) objective to the point at which children no longer view the subject as purposeful – except in as far as it satisfies the teacher's (adult) aims.

STOP AND THINK

▶ If their parents or carers asked them what they did in maths today, what would the children in your class say?

▶ Have you ever had a child tell you (or imply) that something you did in maths was interesting? ... has anyone ever said (or implied) that it will be *useful* to them?

The need for a purpose is clear, I hope, but the thinking opportunity above illustrates one more important point. Have you ever had a child saying that a mathematical idea will be useful to him or her? I have taught hundreds of children and teacher education students and I have never experienced this. What happens often though is that they say how *interesting* the ideas are. Contrary to the popular view, I see no reason for justifying the teaching of maths on the basis that it will be useful to them. Note that I am not saying that it will *not* be useful to them – just that this should not be its *raison d'être*. Studies suggest that what is crucial is that children can see how mathematics relates to situations; be they real (adult) ones, imaginary (play) ones or purely mathematical ones (how mathematical ideas build on each other). The important point is the meaning that children see in a situation; not that this situation relates to any adult sense of meaning and everyday use. Children who experience maths in meaningful (to them) contexts will be more likely to develop a form of mathematical knowledge that they can make use of later than those children who are forced into using so called 'real' contexts because we (the adults) think that it is *directly* useful to them.

Unfortunately, tasks which are purposeful in this sense are not necessarily sufficient. As Ainley et al. point out, there is a 'planning paradox' in that tasks may be made more interesting by opening them up so that children can take control of what is done, but that this means it is less likely that they will address the objectives outlined in the curriculum. Conversely, closing the tasks down to focus on objectives tends to mean that children are less able to take ownership over the task, with a subsequent loss in interest. The trick, of course, is to create tasks that have a clear purpose for the children, but which *force them to engage in the curriculum objective in achieving this*.

KEY IDEA

■ Mathematical activity is most likely to be purposeful when tasks are designed so that:

1 children have something meaningful to 'do'; and

2 in doing it, children come to see how the mathematics operates and how it is used to complete the task.

Having established these ideas in principle we need now to consider how they can be achieved in practice. I suggest three areas that we might consider: setting all work in the context of a problem; creating a need to communicate; and recording mathematical work in different ways.

a) Setting all work in a 'problematic' context

Since mathematics is fundamentally about solving problems, if we want to 'do' maths then we must have problems to solve. In Chapter 2 I made it clear that teaching which works on 'acquiring' a mathematical idea or skill before learning to 'apply' it (demonstrate and practice) tends to result in learners who develop less useful forms of mathematical knowledge. The knowledge is isolated and instrumental rather than connected and relational – and the learners often see little point in the subject, failing to make use of their knowledge in new situations later on. What we want is for learners to learn mathematics *as* problem solving and to develop (useful forms of) mathematical knowledge in doing so.

The difficulty here is that this approach seems daunting. Can we really set all our work in a problem-based form? Doesn't this mean rewriting the curriculum and developing many new tasks? My view is that it need not. For me, 'problem' might better be substituted for 'enquiry'. My aim is that whenever learners engage in mathematics we present it in ways that pose some kind of enquiry. We may sometimes 'do problems' or 'tackle an investigation', but we *always* take a problematic and investigative stance whatever we are doing.

PRACTICAL EXAMPLE

Mei's Year 2 class is working on categorising 2D shapes. The objective in the curriculum planning says that the children should learn to 'sort a set of shapes according to their properties'. Last year Mei got the children to take plastic shapes and to work in groups sorting them into 'families' according to the number of sides, the number of corners and whether sides were straight or curved. Each time the children drew a record of the shapes before resorting.

This year, Mei asks the children to choose one shape from the set and then to draw their own shapes that are either 'in' *or just not* 'in' the same family. The task is to challenge other children, at the end, to establish which shapes do and do not belong. For example, one child chooses an oblong and then draws another 'in' the set. His next shape though has four sides but they do not quite connect in one corner. For another one he deliberately makes one of the sides slightly curved. The challenge is to make the 'not quite in' shapes as close as possible to the original one. Of course, in doing so, the children need to come to some understanding about the properties of the original shape.

At the end the drawings are shared and a discussion ensues about which shapes are in and which out … and what the defining properties are!

In the example above, Mei has tried to capture the properties of a purposeful task. First there is something meaningful to do – to create some 'not quite in' shapes which will catch other children out. It's a game of sorts. To do this successfully, the children have to come to understand the mathematics. In fact they will need to develop a good understanding of the notion of properties since the idea of 'in' or 'not in' forces it. The children are likely to both understand how the mathematics (shape-properties) works and understand how this idea relates to completing the task (how it is useful). Finally, it is set in a problematic context ('how can we catch people out?'; 'what makes a shape belong?') and is likely to promote a sense of enquiry therefore.

One feature of Mei's example is that the task is not defined too fully. One could imagine children asking 'am I allowed to …?'. It is this very sense of imprecision that makes it powerful. Children have to make decisions and explore the implications of these – a very mathematical process to engage in encouraging conjecture and exploration.

David Fielker (1997) identifies several similar strategies that are useful for turning routine problems into more purposeful ones. The book is well worth reading in full, but in summary some of the things he suggests are:

- **Vagueness** – leaving room for children to interpret the problem in different ways and thus explore different aspects of it. For example, in finding ways to make 10, do not specify that you can only use two numbers … or only positive numbers. If children ask whether 1 + 1 + 8 or 12 – 2 are allowed, respond by saying 'I don't know; what happens if they are?'

- **Completeness** – asking children to find *all* the examples of something rather than just some of them; for example, finding all the ways to make 10.

- **Back to front** – provide an answer and ask for possible questions. The classic example is 'the answer's 10: what is the question?' but many other contexts are possible … 'the shape has all opposite sides parallel: what might it be?'; 'prime numbers don't: don't what?' etc.

- **Change something** – take a problem that is familiar and change one or more of its features. For example, square numbers can be drawn as growing square arrangements of dots; triangular numbers can be drawn as growing triangular arrangements of dots. What might pentagonal, or hexagonal numbers look like? Can you find some?

More fundamentally, simply turning all your lesson objectives around into questions, and trying to find something problematic to think about, will immediately make your lessons enquiry-based. Here are a few examples to get you started (and see too the excellent book by Devon's primary mathematics team which does this for the whole curriculum – listed in Further Reading at the end of this chapter).

PRACTICAL EXAMPLES

(F) Find shapes which are **not** square, round …

might become …

M Mixup **always** *gets things wrong. How would he sort these shapes?*

(Y2) Understand the function of zero as a place-holder in two-digit numbers.

might become …

What do zeros do in different numbers? How could you explain this to someone who didn't know?

(Y4) Round any two- or three-digit number to the nearest 10 or 100.

might become …

What are the rules for rounding numbers? Are they good ones, and why?

(Y6) Continue to know by heart all multiplication facts up to 10 x 10.

might become …

Which multiplication facts are the tricky ones, and why? What tips can you offer for learning them?

KEY IDEA

- All lessons can be framed in problematic or investigative ways by reorganising the objective into a statement or question to explore.

b) Creating a need to communicate

One thing that strikes me about the discussions that tend to take place in classrooms is how different they are from discussions that take place outside it. Of course, this is completely reasonable – classroom discussions can never be 'natural' because of the management role that the teacher has to adopt. I believe one aspect of this difference is very significant though and, what is more, that it could be changed. This is the extent to which there is a *need* to communicate.

Were you and I to engage in a discussion it would be because we wanted to resolve something. We would talk because we were trying to make sense of the idea together and to negotiate it. The need to communicate drives the talking and thinking – as Chapter 3 explained. In classrooms things are often different. Children talk because the teacher wants simply to hear what they have to say so others can remember it. I emphasise that this is not automatically a bad thing and will very often be useful, but it reflects the kind of 'transmission' model of learning outlined previously, based on understanding as individual and absolute. Taking the other perspective on understanding, then, given that the need to communicate is a fundamental characteristic of everyday discussion, it would seem like a good idea to try to ensure that this is also a feature of classroom talk where possible.

Each of the three sections of the lesson requires this treatment. In the introduction, setting lessons in problematic contexts, as described in the last section, creates at least a good opportunity for meaningful communication. Children can readily be given a chance to voice their initial points of view about the problem and to respond to the ideas which others put forward. In the middle section, the need for communication will come from the task set and the groupings used – issues I address later.

So what about the ends of lessons; the so-called 'plenary' where children are meant to come together to review learning? How can we go about creating this kind of need for communication? Interestingly, inspection evidence and anecdotal evidence from teachers indicates that this is often the least well managed and least profitable section of the lesson, suggesting that it is particularly difficult to achieve a purposeful ending. In my view, two issues tend to obscure purposeful communication in the plenary of a lesson: *preparation* and *common understanding*.

By *preparation* I am referring to the way in which the teacher has prepared children to come to the plenary, or not as the case may be. It is an obvious thing to say that if we want children to think and talk then they need something purposeful to think and talk *about*. Yet, in my experience, this appears to be less obvious in practice, with little attention given to what children are bringing to a plenary to discuss. All too often, the plenary becomes simply a sharing event where children talk about what they have done or agree (always agree!) with the teacher about what they have learnt.

Common understanding refers to the idea that often children seem to be being asked about things that they have already explored together. Now if I go to the pub and ask my friends if they saw last night's soap/documentary/film and they all say yes, I am left with little to talk about other than to agree a few things about what we liked best. It is when one of us has an experience that the others have not had that a proper discussion ensues. The same is true of classrooms. If we have all been adding two-digit numbers and all done so fairly successfully, there is likely to be little to talk about. On the other hand, if we have had different things to do then there is a reason to talk.

KEY IDEA

- By preparing the children in advance to bring a range of different ideas or objects to the plenary, and deliberately ensuring that other children *do not* already know about them, we can make the plenary more purposeful.

Note that this idea follows on nicely from the notion of framing lessons in problematic and investigative ways, discussed above, since children can bring their own solutions to the plenary. Alternative approaches to the plenary might include the following therefore.

PRACTICAL EXAMPLES

▶ Split a task up into sub-tasks that need to be brought together again for a full picture to emerge.

Example: exploring prime numbers. Split the class into groups and give each group a set of numbers between 0 and 100 to investigate (0–10, 11–20, 21–30 etc.). Then bring them together for the full story.

▶ Provide a choice for children in terms of the questions they tackle in a task so they don't all do the same ones.

Example: adding two-digit numbers. Instead of a sheet of addition problems for everyone, provide two lists of numbers. Children repeatedly choose any number from each list to add together. Include some particular ones (a negative, or a decimal fraction perhaps) to challenge the more able. Ask children to pick numbers that they might find especially challenging, or particularly easy, and then to choose one to talk about in the plenary.

▶ Split the class in two, asking each half to tackle different topics over two days. After the first lesson get children to provide advice to the other group on how best to tackle their task tomorrow.

Example: rounding and estimating. Half the class are working on rounding numbers. In the last five minutes of the main section, children think of 'advice' to offer the other half of the class about how to round, and 'teach' them this in the plenary. Meanwhile, the second half do the same with estimating – the topic they covered today. Tomorrow the halves swap topics.

▶ Pick children who have found novel approaches, or something else worth seeing during the main part of the lesson, to give a short 'masterclass' in the plenary.

Example: Dwayne (5) has worked out that it's more efficient to count on from the larger number in addition. Many others have not yet realised this. The teacher cues him up to tell the others and briefly rehearses what he might say. She then dresses him up with a gown and pointing stick ready for the 'masterclass'!

▶ Ten minutes before finishing, ask children themselves to choose 'something special that others won't know about' to talk about in the plenary. For variations …

    ▶ Take turns for groups to have to choose the special thing and to lead the discussion.

    ▶ Allow things that are *not* true as well as those that are and encourage children to try to con each other (always revealing the truth at the end!). 'We've found a multiple of ten ending in five!' … The audience has to argue for or against.

    ▶ Encourage children not just to tell others about their ideas, but to set the class 'test questions' to see if they have understood it together and can use it themselves.

Finally, it is worth pointing out that it is not always appropriate to hold a class plenary and that there are other ways to share and distribute class understanding. One way is to use 'jigsawing'. This is useful when groups have been working either on the same task, or related tasks. Children create new 'teams' composed of at least one member of the original groups. So, if four original groups (A, B, C and D) had four in each (AAAA, BBBB, CCCC, DDDD) then the new teams would be made up of ABCD, ABCD, ABCD, ABCD. These teams then visit each table where the original groups had been working (perhaps with work left out) and whoever is the 'home' member (i.e. the one who originally worked there) has the task of explaining what that group did. The others can, of course, ask questions and so on.

This, I promise you, is easier to do than to explain on paper! The simplest way in practice is to start with four groups and to get at least one or two people from each one to stand in a corner of the room to form the four new teams. Its great strength is in the way it forces children to talk about their work, and with a bit of careful tweaking also allows you to control who does the talking (useful if you have children who rarely speak in the class setting).

c) Recording mathematical work in different ways

Of all subjects mathematics seems to be the one which falls back on standard forms of recording. Maths and exercise books seem almost as inseparable as cheese and biscuits or Morecombe and Wise. In English there is usually a clear distinction between drafting and presenting. By adopting the same distinction in maths we might create more purpose for children's work and, subsequently, more to communicate about. Children are likely to need to work in exercise books in order to carry out mathematical activity – jottings, workings-out, diagrams and so on – and these should be valued and shared. But they should also be asked to think about different ways to record and to publish their work. Presenting maths in novel ways, and requiring more structured 'publishing', can help in several respects by:

- motivating children to want to act mathematically;

- helping them to make mathematical meaning clear to (and with) others (and hence to themselves);

- modelling good practice;

- making clear what professional mathematicians do;

- providing a purpose for mathematical work and something to discuss.

Examples of some approaches to take are as follows.

PRACTICAL EXAMPLES

▶ Instead of providing worksheets with, say, ten problems to work out, provide just the first three and then ask children to create some more for other children 'that tackle the same mathematical idea' … and work out what the answers would be!

▶ Give out worksheets *without* telling children what to do with them. Get children to discuss what they think the sheet is about, and what must be done.

▶ Ask children to choose just three or four questions from a sheet of ten and complete them. Then get them to *annotate* their responses to show what they were thinking about as they did them and how they were done.

- ▶ Challenge children to create their own textbook pages for another child. The page should include sections explaining the mathematical ideas involved and then some questions that test the other child's understanding. Think how questions may be graded to get progressively harder.

- ▶ Present children with worksheets that you have completed yourself, deliberately getting some questions wrong. Ask them to mark the work as if it was another child's and to think of constructive feedback to give to them. By making the errors systematic, you can model common misconceptions and errors for children.

- ▶ Have a 'top tips' noticeboard on the classroom wall where children can post mathematical advice to each other.

- ▶ Professional mathematicians publish papers in journals. Find some electronic journals on the web and look at them. Talk about the format and the style and then get children to publish their own 'maths journals' as a class, discussing carefully what should be included. Present these to another class.

- ▶ Hold a mathematics conference. Children work in small groups to prepare a poster presentation about some mathematical ideas, then invite another class (or parents!) and 'present' their posters. If you have access to the hall, put the posters up and let an invited audience circulate round them, perhaps leaving comments and questions on A3 sheets pinned up next to the poster.

 KEY IDEA

- ■ Presenting and recording mathematics in novel ways can help to motivate children, improve their understanding and provide a purpose for their mathematical work.

Asking and responding to questions

We have already noted that managing the interaction between a group of thirty or more children and yourself is a demanding task. The teacher constantly treads a tightrope between letting the discussion drift without direction and closing it down too much – both of which lead to inattention and potential disruption on the part of the children.

In this section I focus on asking and responding to questions – both of which work in conjunction to keep mathematical discourse at the forefront of the interaction.

a) Asking questions

A good deal of attention has been given in the past to asking mathematical questions. Questions generally serve three purposes. They:

1 act simply as management tools to control children's behaviour (*who can sit still, put their hand up and tell me what …?*);

2 evaluate children's thinking (*does anyone know what … is?*);

3 promote mathematical thinking (*what might be some different ways to …?*).

Though teachers need to use all three of these for different purposes, my focus is on the last. In particular, if we want children to adopt a mathematical discourse – to act and talk mathematically – we need to ask questions that promote different forms of mathematical thinking. Examples might include the following; ideally, we want to use a range from each group.

PRACTICAL EXAMPLES

Representing mathematical ideas …

■ *What could you show me/draw for me?*

■ *Can you draw a diagram/picture?*

■ *Can you teach that to your partner?*

■ *Can you write that in words for me?*

■ *Can you think of a problem that uses …?*

Classifying mathematical ideas …

■ *Can you see a pattern?*

■ *What connections can you see?*

■ *What might be the same as/different from …?*

■ *Which ones belong to the same set/group/family?*

■ *Which is the odd one out?*

Generalising …

■ *What always seems to happen?*

■ *Will that work every time?*

■ *Can you see the connection between …?*

■ *Can you find one that doesn't do that/work?*

■ *Is there a rule for this?*

Calculating/computing …

■ *Can you find a way to work out …?*

■ *What other ways are there to …?*

▶

PRACTICAL EXAMPLES CONTINUED

- *Is there a quick way?*

- *Will that always get the right answer?*

Conjecturing ...

- *Can you guess what will happen?*

- *Will it be the same/different this time?*

- *What do you think is happening?*

- *What would happen if we ...?*

- *What do you think the rule might be?*

Proving ...

- *How sure are you of that?*

- *What would you say if I disagreed?*

- *Can you convince me?*

- *Can you show me that it **definitely** will/will not?*

- *What makes you so sure about ...?*

b) Responding to questions

As well as asking questions we also need to think carefully about how we *respond* to children's answers. As we saw in the last chapter, the response is at least as important as the question and we want to try to avoid:

- always ending up in the IRF pattern;

- becoming judge and jury by over-evaluating children's responses;

- '(in)appropriating' children's responses for our own teaching;

- preventing the discussion from flowing by always interrupting it.

What tends to happen when we allow ourselves to fall into these patterns is that we kill off the mathematical thinking that might take place. The key to this mathematical homicide is, as I have pointed out, in the discourses of the classroom and the mathematics. In particular it is affected by the strongest driving force in the classroom discourse, namely the need for children to match their responses to those that the teacher wants to see – to get things 'right' in other words. This mutual alignment of responses may look and feel like an effective learning environment because everyone is giving the right answers to questions – there is no conflict so I must be teaching effectively. But it is the classroom discourse that is running smoothly; because everyone is fitting into the classroom *norms*. From a mathematical point of view little is likely to be happening. Every time children begin to think about an idea we can tend to take it over and cut off their opportunity to think about it.

The main culprit in this curtailing of children's thinking is the evaluation of their responses and particularly in the way we tend to demonstrate to everyone whether an answer is right or wrong too quickly.

KEY IDEA

■ Because the classroom discourse is largely about children aligning themselves with the teacher's thoughts, children will stop thinking about an idea as soon as they know what is 'right'.

In principle, changing this is easy; we simply need to stop ourselves from revealing the 'right', or desired, answer immediately all the time. Instead, we want to find responses that encourage the children themselves to evaluate answers so that they remain engaged in the mathematics going on. As I pointed out in Chapter 4, we want the focus to be on whether the maths is *accurate*, not on whether it is 'right' in the teacher's eyes. And, uniquely, mathematics has this power; to be its own authority. Children do not need the teacher to judge right from wrong when the mathematics itself can lead them to the accurate conclusion.

IN YOUR CLASSROOM

All of the following cues reveal the accuracy of an answer.

▶ Which ones do you habitually use?

  ■ 'well done'; 'good'; 'ok'; 'smashing'; 'lovely' etc.

  ■ smiling

  ■ nodding

  ■ putting thumbs up

  ■ not recording answers on the board (often only inaccurate answers are recorded so that they can be examined by the class)

  ■ turning quickly to the next question

▶ Are there others that you can catch yourself using too?

So is it true that we should not smile (at least until Christmas!) or nod our heads? No, of course not; I recommend plenty of smiling to remind children that maths should be enjoyable. But it is the intent that matters. If you *always* smile at accurate answers and never at inaccurate ones, or more often write inaccurate ones on the board and never do so with accurate ones, then children soon learn to read these cues as mathematical executioners – 'he's smiled folks, we can stop thinking about that one'. It is the habitual nature of these actions which labels them … and makes them hard to change! And of course, much of the time they are fine and will be used to keep the classroom interaction flowing nicely, as we must do. To avoid killing-off thinking too much though we need different response strategies too.

PRACTICAL EXAMPLES

▶ Replace positive verbal cues ('good', 'well done' etc.) with more neutral responses:

■ 'thank you'

■ 'that's a good start'

■ 'ok, what else?'

■ 'interesting, thanks'

■ 'ok, any others?'

■ 'what do people think?'

▶ Avoid smiling; keep your face neutral, and do so for both inaccurate and accurate answers.

▶ Collect inaccurate *and* accurate answers on the board for discussion.

▶ Ask children to explain how they got their answers when they are accurate *and* when they are inaccurate.

Replacing affirming responses with more neutral ones sends out the message that it is the children's responsibility to evaluate the accuracy of the mathematics – and to keep thinking about it. A very useful strategy is to collect a number of answers together, only one of which is accurate, and then to ask children to justify which it is. You can:

■ ask the child who gave each answer to justify its accuracy;

■ ask other children to choose the accurate one and justify their choice;

■ vote on them, explaining the reason for their votes;

■ play 'call my bluff' and ask children to try to justify even the inaccurate ones – great fun, particularly if you have some more able children in the class!

As well as encouraging more extended thinking, these kinds of responses also promote two fundamental ideas in mathematics: **conjecture** and **proof**. Conjecture refers to making statements about what we believe to be accurate; 'I think that …' statements, for example. Proof tends to get less attention, but is absolutely central to mathematics, since the whole subject is fundamentally about demonstrating how and why ideas are interconnected. At primary level it is perhaps better thought of as children engaging in *careful justification*; convincing someone else that their idea is accurate and demonstrating why it is so. Done regularly, and with significance, children will develop their ability to reason mathematically, using the idea of '*if this is true, then this must be true*' that characterises deductive reasoning.

KEY IDEAS

- In responding to children's answers we should try to keep the mathematics alive by not revealing the accurate answer too quickly.

- The aim should be to encourage children to evaluate the accuracy of responses and to justify their decisions.

- Doing so provides the vehicle for developing important mathematical approaches such as conjecture and proof.

A final word on responding to questions. As I have pointed out, much of our interaction with children is *habitual*, as it should be to allow us to think about other things while we do it. Whilst this is useful, it does mean that it can be hard to change, and whilst all the suggestions above look simple they can be very hard to effect in practice. The first step is to catch your habitual actions. Then, when you can catch them before you do them, you are in a position to choose to change.

Encouraging children to talk clearly and accurately

Though English classrooms are full of talk, more often than not it is largely unstructured and informal. As we saw in the last chapter, children themselves are frequently unhappy with the difficulties they have in following classroom discussion. In essence, talking tends to be seen as 'something to listen to' not as a means of making sense in its own right. Ideally, we should try to ensure that:

- children see talking as part of the 'work' to be carried out – as a means of learning;

- they learn to talk clearly and accurately about mathematical ideas;

- everyone gets a chance to talk and to be part of a joint effort in making meaning and understanding together.

I have already mentioned above that children are usually seeking ways to match their answers to those that they think the teacher is looking for. Note that this is unlikely to be a deliberate choice on the part of the children; it is one of the norms of human interaction, particularly when one of the participants (the teacher in this case) is a figure of authority. In social circumstances we all tend to give answers that 'fit' the expectations of the situation. That is why when we ask someone how they are feeling today we expect a cheery 'fine thanks', or at most a 'not too bad', but not an in depth analysis of their real state of health.

The mutual alignment of people's interaction in this way is, of course, necessary most of the time. But in classrooms, when we have engineered a class interaction, we want *learning conversations*, not just social conversations. The purpose of the discussion taking place should be to challenge current thinking and to hear new ideas and approaches. We want to break out of the social pattern so that children expect to have to articulate fully what they mean and potentially be challenged on it. This will mean that they struggle to express themselves some of the time and we may occasionally need to be strong in holding back from (in)appropriating their responses in order to rescue them – within a supportive environment, of course. In passing, I would point out that we seem happy to let children struggle (suitably) with written work, but leap in to save them as soon as talking becomes difficult. This illustrates just what I mean about the way in which talking is viewed in our classrooms.

KEY IDEAS

- Whole class interaction is a learning conversation, not a social conversation, and should help children to get better at articulating their ideas and challenging those of others.

- This may feel uncomfortable at first, and children will need to learn that they may not say the right thing straight away, but that you will give them time to articulate their thinking.

The following practical examples show how you might make changes to your teaching in respect of the three bullet points above: seeing talking as 'work'; learning to talk clearly and accurately; and giving everyone a chance to be involved.

PRACTICAL EXAMPLES

Seeing talking as 'work'

- Praise effective talking on a regular basis and make clear that *you* view it as work.

- Plan lessons in which there is no written product and make clear to the children that you will be expecting them to talk about their work at the plenary.

- Encourage children when they struggle to articulate an idea and praise them for persevering.

- Make clear to children that they are jointly responsible for making new ideas together by talking – say 'can we make sense of this together?' rather than 'who knows how/why …?'.

- Where an idea seems to be understood by one group, but not by others, try creating a '*learning network*'. Children stand up and move from person to person teaching and learning with each other. '***Everyone*** *must understand together in two minutes time*'. '*Once **you** understand, pass it on …*'.

- Notice times when children successfully make sense of an idea together and point this out to them.

PRACTICAL EXAMPLES

Learning to talk clearly and accurately

Much of the time it is the teacher who interferes with children's attempts to talk clearly and accurately. Albeit for superficially supportive reasons, teachers often interrupt, take over or manipulate responses to 'help' the child. Try to avoid too much help by:

■ Being patient and allowing children time to construct their answers.

■ Withdrawing to the side of the group and expecting speakers to talk to the other children, not just you.

■ Staying silent yourself and simply pointing to the next speaker (to reduce your role in the evaluation of the ideas being offered).

■ Making clear that it is ok to try to say something and not yet be able to – say 'I don't *yet* understand you' (emphasising 'yet' to imply that making meaning clear takes time and effort) and 'can anyone else help?'.

■ Expecting clear responses – ask the other children if they can all hear and get the speaker to say it again if not.

■ Expecting articulate responses – say 'I don't understand what you mean *yet*; I'll come back to you in a minute' and expect them to try again.

■ Asking other children if they understand *yet* and getting them to support the talker – say 'can anyone add anything that might help?'.

■ Focusing on the act of saying something clearly, perhaps by asking children to say again clearly something that they have struggled to articulate the first time.

■ Making clear that a full explanation is a joint venture that will take time – say 'let's try to understand this together'; 'who can get us started?'; 'can anyone add anything now?'; 'what do people think about that?' etc.

■ Asking children to *rehearse* responses in pairs before speaking; or getting groups to *plan* what they will say just before the plenary starts.

PRACTICAL EXAMPLES

Involving everyone

You can help children to get involved in whole class discussions by:

- Sitting the children in a circle, or a horseshoe so that they can direct their talk at each other and not just at you.

- Slowing things down – remember, 'pace' may be important in some respects, but thinking takes time.

- Providing opportunities to rehearse (in pairs) before actually speaking.

- Working in small groups for a few minutes where the task is to 'make sure *everyone* understands'.

- Choosing individuals to respond, but giving them thinking time by asking another question to someone else first.

- Asking for contributions towards the answer, not expecting complete responses – ask 'can you tell me anything about …?'.

- Emphasising that the answer will be constructed from a number of responses and not expecting complete answers immediately – say 'you've made a good start there, who can carry on now?'.

- Appointing a child as 'temporary chair' to manage a discussion whilst you take a back seat (literally!).

Using a 'magic microphone' so that only the child who holds it can speak, helps to manage the discussion too. A more structured approach is to give them 'talking tokens' (lollipop sticks or counters). Every time someone says something they have to give up a token. You can then:

- Stop individuals dominating the discussion by controlling the number of tokens.

- Require quieter children to contribute by (gently) expecting everyone to use at least one (or all) of their tokens.

- Use coloured tokens to indicate different aspects of mathematical discussion (questions, statements, conjectures, proofs etc.) which children must take part in.

- Hold and give up tokens yourself so that children know that they must take responsibility for managing the discussion without you.

Finally, the idea of *proof* was mentioned earlier in this chapter. Proof gives maths its own authority to judge the accurate from the inaccurate since to prove something in maths is to show that it must be the case (if only in as far as it can be deduced logically from an agreed starting point). By focusing on the idea of 'convincing other people' we can create a need for communication to be clear and accurate. Children may be more likely to accept the need to develop this clarity if they perceive it as a requirement of the mathematics itself, rather than simply because the teacher asks them to. The message is 'you *need* to be clear to make sense' not 'you need to be clear because I say so'!

Summary

- ■ Overcoming the challenges of whole class interactive teaching is challenging because many of the dilemmas teachers face are systemic, resulting from the way classrooms operate.

- ► Briefly review the chapter and consider which of the issues that have been raised seem to resonate with your own experiences.

- ■ Even within these constraints we can free up children to think about the mathematical discourse by adopting a problematic/investigative stance to all maths work and by trying to create a need to communicate about mathematical ideas.

- ► What sorts of challenges does this raise for you in your teaching context? How would the resources you currently use help or hinder this change in approach?

- ■ Asking and responding to questions is a key issue in promoting mathematical thinking through interactive teaching.

- ► What changes, if any, can you make to the way in which you ask/respond to questions? Can you identify things that you currently do which are habitual and hard to change?

- ■ Encouraging children to talk clearly can demand a change in attitudes towards talk so that it is seen as part of mathematics work. Talking can also be difficult and children need to feel free to make mistakes in what they say.

- ► How is talk viewed in your classroom and what might you change to help children to talk more clearly and effectively?

📖 Further reading

Devon County Council (Primary mathematics team) (2005) *Using and applying in every maths lesson: Ideas for the primary classroom.* Exeter: DCS publications.
Fielker, D. (1997) *Extending Mathematical Ability Through Whole Class Teaching.* London: Hodder and Stoughton.

CHAPTER 6

Starting points for interactive number work

This chapter will …

■ illustrate the ideas that have been discussed in the book so far through two extended 'lesson examples' in the context of number;

■ give examples of possible dialogue between teachers and children to illustrate how the lesson might appear in practice;

■ provide starting points for other number activities, each modelling different approaches from Chapter 5.

In discussing interactive teaching and what it entails, I have tried to illustrate not just what might be done but also why and how it should be done, with examples provided along the way of questions, responses, tasks and so on. Because of the linear nature of a book, these have inevitably been separated from each other in order to discuss each topic in turn. This chapter aims to bring them back together again and to show how they can work in harmony to support planning for more interactive teaching of number.

In order to balance examples that provide some depth with a sufficient breadth of ideas, I start with two fairly extended outlines of how a lesson might look. I then give a series of shorter, more concise, starting points for rich interaction in the context of number, covering Key Stages 1 and 2.

Though not complete 'lesson plans', each extended example illustrates:

■ the purpose from the adult's perspective in the form of a *learning 'centre-point'* for the lesson;

■ the purpose from the children's perspective in the form of a *purposeful task*;

■ a suggestion for getting each lesson *started*, including *initiating questions* you might ask and *teaching points* to bear in mind;

■ potential *follow-up questions* to develop children's mathematical thinking;

■ a *main task* for children to carry out;

■ suggested *preparation for the plenary* to ensure children come to this ready to contribute meaningfully;

■ a *commentary* describing the intent behind each suggestion.

In addition to these planning points, one small section of each example (marked in the plan with a heavy line ▬▬▬▬▬▬▬) is considered in terms of how interaction between teacher and children might 'look'. Though imaginary, I hope these snippets of dialogue will help you to get a sense of how the interaction might feel in practice.

Example lesson outline 1: Rounding whole numbers (Year 5)

Planning points	Commentary
Learning centre-point: Round any two-, three- or four-digit number to the nearest 10, 100 or 1000.	A typical objective taken from the numeracy curriculum.
Purposeful task: Create a page for a maths textbook on rounding numbers to 10, 100 and 1000.	The lesson assumes that the children already have a reasonable understanding of the topic. The task will require them to (re)articulate and represent the way in which rounding works.
Getting started: **Teaching point:** Sit children in a horseshoe. Remember to use neutral responses to answers to encourage children to keep thinking creatively. ▲ *'These numbers have already been rounded. Were they rounded to the nearest 10, 100, or 1000?'* 310 3500 6000 ▲ *'For each one, what might the original number have been before rounding?'*	The problem is presented **back to front** and there is a deliberate element of **vagueness** here. 3500 could have been rounded to the nearest 100 or the nearest 10 if the original number was 3448, say. Similarly, 6000 could have been rounded to the nearest 10, 100 or 1000 if the starting number had been 6002.
Teaching point: Look for **completeness** – find *all* the possibilities.	A **range of answers** is possible and the range itself will depend on the point above. For example, if 3500 was rounded to the nearest 100, then all numbers in the range 3450–3549 would be possible; if to the nearest 10, then only 3495–3504 are possible ... and even this implies whole numbers. Which decimal fractions (3504.99999?) would count adds lots of complexity!

Follow-up questions ...
▲ *'How sure are you? Can you convince us?'*
▲ *'What rules are you following to work it out?'*
▲ *'Can you give us a procedure for working these out?'*
	Focus on:
	  ■ **proof**
	  ■ **generalisation**
	  ■ **procedures**
	
	These questions will help the class to articulate the procedures for rounding numbers.

▶

Example lesson outline 1: Rounding whole numbers (Year 5) continued

Planning points	Commentary
Check that the procedures work by trying them on some other numbers like 583 and 2848. Remember to include 'special case' examples ending in 5. **Teaching point:** Remember to step back from judging the responses yourself. Let the children decide if they are accurate or not.	
The main task: Show the children some examples of pages from textbooks and discuss the kind of layout they have. **Focus on:** ■ clarity of explanation ■ diagrams and visual layout ■ examples ■ practice questions, including 'special cases' Set children to work in pairs or threes, planning and producing a textbook page.	You might provide a **writing frame** for this – see the photocopiable on page 130. Encourage children to think about: ■ what they can **draw** as well as say ■ **examples** that illustrate 'easy' ones, 'hard' ones and 'special cases'
Preparation for the plenary: Five minutes before the plenary, walk around the room and choose three examples that model effective 'explanation' of the key ideas. Ask these children to prepare to show their examples to the class.	Help children to **prepare** to talk by allowing them five minutes to practise what they are going to say.
In the plenary: Ask the class to work in their pairs/threes and to evaluate the three example pages. ▲ *'What are the strengths?'* ▲ *'How could they be developed?'* Finish with pairs/threes planning improvements to their own textbook pages in a future lesson.	Hold back from too much comment yourself. Ask a child to 'chair' the discussion.

Interaction in practice … Rounding (Year 5)

Getting started …

T: Have a look at these numbers (writes 310, 3500 and 6000 on the board). If I tell you that they've all been rounded in some way, can you tell me how? Talk to your neighbour.

[Paired discussion …]

T: OK. What can anyone tell me?

Ch1:   That one's ten.

T: Ten? I don't know what you mean yet. Can you say more?

Ch1:   They've been rounded to ten … well the 310 has.

[Teacher nods to indicate that she has heard this and then gestures for other responses.]

Ch2:   That one [indicates 6000] is to the nearest 1000.

Ch3:   Yeah, thousand … the six thousand one is thousands.

T: What do others think?

[General agreement]

T: Can anyone say something else then?

Ch4:   [Quietly, near the front] The 6000 has been rounded to 1000 and the 3500 is to 100.

T: Did everyone hear that?

All: No …

T: Can you talk to everyone?

Ch4:   [More clearly] The 6000 has been rounded to 1000 and the 3500 is to 100.

T: What do people think?

[General agreement]

T: OK, we all seem to agree. What I want you to think about is whether it is possible to *disagree* with this. Can you discuss it again. I want you *not* to agree.

[Paired discussion for a minute …]

T: [Interrupting] … I'm getting the feeling, listening to you, that you can't find a way to disagree. What I want you to do then is to think about how this might be rounded [writes 3496 on the board]. See if that helps you …

[Paired discussion again …]

Ch5:   [Calling out] … it could go either way.

Ch6: Yes, 10 or 100. It's either 3500 or … [thinks] well it's always 3500 but it could be 10 or 100 …

T: [Waits to see if anything else is said … then] I'm not clear yet.

Ch6: What I mean is that you can round it to 10 or 100. But they'll both go to 3500.

T: What do people think about that?

Ch5: I think she means that the 6 could go up to 10, which would be 3500, or the 96 could go up to 100 which would be 3500, again.

[Teacher nods, but says nothing. Indicates for other responses with raised palms and moves to the side.]

Ch7: Yes. It could be either. Or to the nearest 1!

Ch5: No. It can't be one. They all end in zero.

Ch8: It can only be 10, or 100.

Ch7: No … if we had started with three four nine nine point a six [3499.6] it would.

[General chatter]

Ch8: You can't use decimals.

[General chatter …]

T: Wow! What do people think about that? Is it ok to use decimals here and to say it was rounded to the nearest one? Talk about it in your pairs again.

[Children chatter and one or two voice their ideas. After a while the general consensus seems to be that it is OK.]

T: OK. We look like we pretty well understand this. Indera, you said that you couldn't use decimals, what do you think now?

Ch8: Yeah, you can. I see it now.

T: OK. Great. Now, what I want you to do is get together in fours and practise explaining it. You've got to make sure that *everyone* in the group understands it and can say it clearly. Use the 6000 example then I'll choose someone to do it.

The nature of the interactions is worth noting in the text above. Though the teacher still dominates the conversation in terms of the number of speaking turns, there are occasions where several children speak in turn without any intervention. Sitting in a horseshoe or circle, holding back from commenting all the time, using open hand gestures and facial expressions to indicate that he/she wants other children to speak, all help the teacher to avoid the kind of IRF domination discussed in Chapter 5. Secondly, note carefully the nature of the teacher's interventions. They are all based on facilitating the discussion and pointing it in new directions – not feedback on children's comments. Most importantly, it is the children who are doing the mathematical thinking and not (overtly) the teacher.

Example lesson outline 2: Solve simple mathematical problems or puzzles (Year 1)

Planning points	Commentary
Learning centre-point: Solve a simple number problem, recognising patterns and relationships.	A typical objective taken from the numeracy curriculum
Purposeful task: The answer is 5. What could **all** the questions have been?	'Find the questions' is a useful and well used task. Here the emphasis is on 'completeness' and finding *all* solutions – at least as far as addition and subtraction are concerned.
Getting started: ▶ *'Watch what I'm doing …'* Start writing a variety of calculations and pictures on the board, all involving 5. e.g. 4 + 1; 1 + 2 + 2; ◆◆ / ◆ ◆ / ◆ ; ●●●●● ; 10 – 5; etc.	The key feature here is **vagueness.** It is the fact that you are *not* being clear about what is happening that engages the children's attention.
▶ *'What do you think might be going on?'*	Notice that saying 'what do you think *might* be going on?' emphasises the tentative nature of the task and makes it easier for children to make suggestions. Compare this to 'what am I doing?' – implying the need to guess a definite, particular answer.
Teaching point: Get the children thinking by being deliberately vague. Stay silent if possible; let the children suggest ideas and see what they say.	
▶ *'Who would like to try drawing something? I'll tell you if it is allowed.'* Without revealing why, accept or reject offers depending on whether they come to 5 or not.	Again, the idea is *not* to talk too much. Staying silent creates an air of mystery and engages thinking.
As children begin to guess the idea of 5, move to a *learning network*.	

▶

Example lesson outline 2: Solve simple mathematical problems or puzzles (Year 1) continued

Planning points	Commentary
▲ *When you know what is going on you've got to explain it to someone else.* *You have two minutes to make sure everyone in the class knows.*	The emphasis here is on *everyone* knowing. This helps to make learning through talking a joint venture and shares out responsibility for understanding amongst the group.
Follow-up questions … ▲ *'What other ways of representing '5' could we have?'* ▲ *'Can you see any patterns here?'* ▲ *'How many do you think there are?'* ▲ *'How might we find out?'*	Note the focus on: **Conjecturing, classifying** and the beginnings of **proving.** You might start to organise the solutions on the board into groups – additions of 2, 3, 4, numbers, subtractions, pictures etc.
The main task: Introduce the idea of finding *all* possible solutions for addition and subtractions. Allocate different tasks to each group. Focus on: ▲ additions of just two numbers ▲ additions of three numbers ▲ additions of four or more numbers ▲ subtractions (probably of just two numbers)	Note that it is impossible, in fact, to write down all solutions – the subtractions alone have infinitely many because of the continuous pattern … 5 – 0, 6 – 1, 7 – 2 etc. Similarly, there are quite a number of ways to use three numbers. This need not matter – we can still encourage children to think about the *process* of finding them all, and discovering it *cannot* be done is as important, mathematically, as discovering it can.
Provide counting objects so that children can group them in different ways to find solutions.	Those who are adding will need five objects; those subtracting will need more than five.
Also provide a large piece of paper and a felt pen to record findings on. Focus on: ■ patterns ■ being systematic ■ recording work in numerals and/or pictures	Note that, although the session is ostensibly about problem solving, children will get lots of practice in adding and subtracting *through* the investigation.

▶

Example lesson outline 2: Solve simple mathematical problems or puzzles (Year 1) continued

Planning points	Commentary
Teaching point: If children ask 'can I ...? [e.g. 'can I do 3 + 2 and 2 + 3?'], resist the temptation to make the decision for them. Instead, ask 'what difference would that make?' and let them choose.	Making decisions in maths is an important idea to develop. In order to be able to make informed decisions, children need to learn to examine their *implication*.
Preparation for the plenary: Ten minutes before the plenary starts, ask each group to review what they have done so far and choose one thing to tell everyone about. Get the group to rehearse what they are going to say, and who is going to say it and to prepare their piece of paper for presentation to the group.	This preparation time is important if children are going to make useful contributions to the plenary.
In the plenary: Let each group feed back in turn, sticking their paper up first to show their recordings. **Teaching point:** Hold back from doing too much talking yourself by recording ideas on the board. If children talk *to you*, gesture towards the class to encourage them to talk to everyone. ▲ *'What have we found?'* ▲ *'What else are we still to find?'*	Focus on what is still to be found out, as well as what has been discovered.
Teaching point: Record the things still to be discovered and display them as questions on a board. Go back to them another time, and/or set them as homework.	It is important to show children that mathematical work often leads to new questions and that these are valued. They need to see that the subject can generate its own questions, which may need extended exploration. So much of school maths happens within an hour that children come to see it as a short term affair. They soon begin to believe that if they cannot do it immediately then it cannot be done and lose the willingness to persevere with it.

Interaction in practice … Problem solving (Year 1)

Plenary:

T: OK, OK, settle down. Let's have you sitting in your groups on the carpet here.

         I want everyone looking this way and listening … OK? Everyone ready?

         Now, who is going to feed back from the first group? Katie?

Ch1:   [Sitting] We were doing the add ones …

T: Hold on Katie. Can everyone hear her?

         [General chorus of 'no']

T: Where could you stand Katie so that we can all hear you? … That's right, come to the front here … OK, off you go again. I'll stick your piece of paper up here.

Ch1:   We done the adding three numbers. We got … [to the teacher] do you want me to tell you or them all?

T: Tell *them* [indicates the class].

Ch1:   We done 1 and 1 and 3 [child indicates record on paper; teacher records 1 + 1 + 3 on board].

         Then we done this one: 1 and 2 and 2. Then we done 1 and 3 and 1, 2 and 1 and 2, 2 and 2 and 1 …

         [Teacher records each answer but groups them according to the numbers used: {1 + 1 + 3} {1 + 3 + 1} and {1 + 2 + 2} {2 + 1 + 2} {2 + 2 + 1}.]

T: OK, thanks Katie. I want you to talk in your groups now about what they've got and what they may not have got.

         [Group discussions]

T: OK. Any ideas?

Ch2:   Those are the same [pointing].

T: Which ones?

Ch2:   Those [indicates the 1, 2, 2 and the 2, 1, 2 patterns].

T: Interesting, what do other people think?

Ch3:   No.

T: Aren't they?

Ch3:   No. Cos one is 1,2, 2 and then 2, 1, 2. It's different.

         [Teacher pulls a puzzled face and gestures with her hands for more ideas.]

Ch4:   Yeah, different.

Ch5:   Different.

[Chorus of 'different' and 'same' from children]

T: OK. Let's see then. If you think they are the same, come to this side of the carpet. If you think they are different, come to the other side of the carpet. [Children shuffle over] That's it. OK, if you don't know, stay in the middle …

Now, talk to a neighbour about your reason. You've got to try to convince us you are right! Middlers, if you decide, shuffle over to the group.

[Small group discussions]

T: Right. Come on Tom, tell us what you think.

Ch6: Same, cos they are the same numbers.

Ch7: [Interrupting] Yeah, but different way. Look they are different.

T: How do you mean?

Ch7: Look, this is 1, 2, 2 and this is 2, 1, 2 … different.

Ch5: That's what I meant before.

Ch8: But they are both 6.

T: I think you mean 5. [To child 7] He's right, they are both 5.

Ch7: Yeah, but the different way round. So it's different.

T: That's true, isn't it. What do you say to that 'samers'?

What do you people in the middle think? Has anyone made up their mind?

… [The interaction continues for a short while]

T: OK, well we've decided that you can think either the same or different, you just get a different number of answers. Now, do you think we've found them *all*?

[No response]

T: Well, look, we have got three of these ones [indicates the 1,2,2 group] and only two of these.

[Pauses to let children talk and moves away from the front to show them they can do so freely. After a while several eager hands go up.]

T: OK, I think a few people can see something missing. Now, don't tell *me*. If you think you can see it, tell people around you. Spread the word!

[Children begin to 'share' idea of the 'missing' 3 + 1 + 1. Growing hubbub ensues.]

Examples of other possible starting points for number

Having presented two examples of lesson outlines, the remainder of this chapter provides a series of starting points for investigating number across Key Stages 1 and 2. Though concise, they offer examples of the kinds of tasks and contexts that might stimulate children's interest in the subject and provide a platform for lively interaction. My aim is to show what is possible – assuming that you will change, adapt, remove and add ideas as you see fit.

Foundation

Learning centre-point	Purposeful task	Interactive opportunities – getting started	Interactive opportunities – plenary
Recognise and use numerals to ten.	**Create a puzzle page** for a class book in which numbers 0–10 are muddled up and need to be reordered correctly.	■ Play Miss or Mr Count (a puppet who miscounts ... children must spot the mistakes). ■ Provide 0–10 number cards to hold; ask children to order themselves on the carpet. ■ Close eyes; two 'numbers' swap place; agree with a partner who has changed. ■ Model 'puzzles' on the board by writing numbers in the wrong order. Talk in pairs about what is wrong. ■ Children work in pairs to create their own 'muddled' number puzzles (either writing their own numerals or gluing in numeral cards).	■ Choose children in advance to share one of their puzzles verbally with the class, reading the numbers out loud – provide practice time. ■ Encourage children to discuss in their pairs how the numbers need to be reordered. ■ Choose examples of children's written puzzles and ask children to evaluate how clearly they have been done.

Extensions:

■ Extend the puzzles to count in different steps ... twos and tens.

■ Extend the puzzles to count backwards as well as forwards.

■ Make the children's puzzles into several small books and send these home for children to try out with their parents, or put them up on display in the school somewhere.

Year 1

Learning centre-point	Purposeful task	Interactive opportunities – getting started	Interactive opportunities – plenary

Understand the operation of addition.	**Research a true/ false statement** about addition and **draw a representation** for a class display board.	■ Present children with an example statement such as 'You can only add with two numbers. It doesn't work with three'. Ask for ideas about the statement, discussing in pairs first.
		■ Focus on *generalising, proving* and *representing* questions:
		  – *'Is it true?... always?'*
		  – *'Give me an example.'*
		  – *'What could you show me?'*
		  – *'How could you convince me?'*
		■ Encourage children to think carefully about examples that demonstrate the idea and about what they could show 'to convince each other'. Focus on pictorial representations as well as numerals.
		■ Provide groups of four with other statements (both true and false) to explore together:
		  – *'Adding zero makes no difference.'*
		  – *'Adding ten doesn't change anything.'*
		  – *'Adding and taking away are opposites.'*
		  – *'You can't make nine with three different numbers.' etc.*
			■ Choose examples prior to the plenary that illustrate clear explanations. Ask children to prepare to explain their ideas when the plenary starts.
			■ Take turns asking questions and showing 'justifications'. Ask listeners to evaluate each group ... 'are you convinced?'
			■ Get each group to think up one or two questions for the rest of the class which will illustrate their idea in practice.

Extensions:

■ 'Publish' children's ideas on a display board. Use folded card with the statement on the outside and the explanation on the inside.

■ Ask children to take their ideas to another class (a year above) and to explain their thinking to an older learner.

Year 2

Learning centre-point	Purposeful task	Interactive opportunities – getting started	Interactive opportunities – plenary
Mental calculation strategies for addition and subtraction.	**Examine a worksheet** and try to work out what mathematical idea it demonstrates. **Create 'advice'** for others completing the sheet.	■ Prior to the lesson, create 'worksheets' of subtraction questions but without instructions at the top (for examples see photocopiable on page 132). Include only a few questions but use them to model particular strategies such as adding 10, bridging 10 or 100, complements to 100 etc. ■ Start in groups of six away from the carpet area. Provide each group with a 'worksheet' to discuss. – *'What mathematics do you think this sheet is about?'* – *'What do you have to do to complete it?'* ■ Come together on the carpet and discuss ideas about addition and subtraction. Let a spokesperson for each group speak in turn and look for connections between ideas. ■ Regroup in pairs to go off to complete the questions and to develop further questions of their own based on the same idea. Ask for 'hard' ones, 'easy' ones and extensions of the same idea.	■ Ten minutes before the plenary, go back to groups of six. Ask the group to develop 'advice for other people doing these questions' and 'one example question' for the class. ■ Allow groups one minute each to present their advice and set their question to the class. Encourage children to manage this discussion themselves and stick to the one minute ruling. ■ Present some general questions that use the strategies discussed and ask children to think about which strategy they might use.

Extensions:

■ Get children to write their own worksheets for each other. This makes them think about the mathematics involved … and saves you time!

■ Make it a general principle that children look carefully at worksheets *before* being told what to do. This focuses them on thinking about the purpose of the sheet and the mathematics involved, rather than just getting it done.

■ If you are giving children worksheets, ask them only to complete questions until they can explain what is going on mathematically. Rather than doing the rest of the questions, ask them to create their own 'really hard ones' and to do them.

■ Ask children who have understood to act as 'personal tutor' for a child who does not yet understand it. Aim to have everyone being tutors by the end of the lesson!

Year 3

Learning centre-point	Purposeful task	Interactive opportunities – getting started	Interactive opportunities – plenary

Use knowledge of number facts and place value to multiply and divide mentally.	Over two days … Coach a group of 'experts' to become 'tomorrow's teachers'.	■ On day one, work with a group whilst others get on with different tasks.
		■ Talk with the group about calculating mentally using multiplication and division.
		■ Ask pairs to become 'experts' in this and prepare 'to teach the class tomorrow'. Also prepare five questions that will test learners' understanding.
		■ Focus on:
		  – what they might *show* to help the group understand
		  – procedures they can demonstrate for carrying out calculations
		■ On day two, start with each pair teaching their ideas to the whole class.
		■ Then allocate one 'expert' per group to work with the rest of the class on their prepared questions.
			■ Discuss, as a class, the quality of the teaching and how well everyone understands the ideas.
			■ Ask the 'experts' to report back on the questions that the group tackled, with group members contributing as appropriate.

Extensions:

■ Choose new groups of children to become experts in future lessons.

■ Make use of ICT by getting the 'expert' groups to use Interactive Teaching Programmes (ITPs) or to create simple PowerPoint presentations for their teaching.

Year 4

Learning centre-point	Purposeful task	Interactive opportunities – getting started	Interactive opportunities – plenary
Develop and refine written methods for multiplying.	**Mark some work** and think about feedback that would help the learner to do better. Develop this to become **critical markers**.	■ Prior to the lesson, produce 'completed worksheets'. These should have both accurate and inaccurate responses on them, perhaps modelling common mistakes (for an example, see photocopiable on page 133). They can also be differentiated to match different children's potentials. ■ Present the class with some problems involving 2-digit × 1-digit multiplications. Collect answers neutrally and then ask children to justify their answer. Discuss 'how the calculation might go wrong'. ■ Present examples of both accurate and inaccurate solutions to other multiplication problems (perhaps modelling those done by members of the class on a prior occasion). Discuss in pairs. – *'What has been done well?'* – *'What has been misunderstood?'* ■ Ask children what they might say/show to the child who had done it in order to help them. Model ways of providing constructive feedback to people. ■ Set children working in groups to 'mark' the worksheets. Each group must prepare a 'tutorial' with the imaginary child to help them develop their thinking. The tutorial can involve example questions, visual models and/or verbal explanations.	■ Five minutes before the plenary, choose two groups to feed back their ideas. Ask them to get ready to show what they would do in their tutorial. ■ In the plenary, take the role of the 'child' who had done the work and role-play the tutorial with both groups in turn. ■ Play 'dumb' and challenge the group to help you understand. ■ Stop from time to time to allow other children to comment on the group's teaching skills and understanding of the topic.

Extensions:

■ Discuss the idea of marking more generally, thinking about 'what sort of feedback is useful for you?'

■ In future lessons, put children in groups marking each other's work and discussing what has gone wrong.

Year 5

Learning centre-point	Purposeful task	Interactive opportunities – getting started	Interactive opportunities – plenary
Order familiar fractions.	**Create a teaching poster** showing how fractions can be ordered.	■ Write $\frac{1}{2}$ on the board. Ask children to call out other fractions. Place them to the right or the left depending on whether they are bigger/smaller than $\frac{1}{2}$. Don't reveal what you are doing. ■ Ask children to guess how you are categorising the fractions, explaining their thinking. Ask others to comment on the ideas. Focus on deducing the relative size using number lines, objects and division. ■ Start afresh, but this time ask for fractions and place them to the left/right depending on their value in relation to $\frac{2}{3}$ ... tell children you have a fraction in your head, but do not write $\frac{2}{3}$ on the board. ■ Ask children to discuss which fraction you are thinking of and to justify their answer. ■ Ask children what they can tell you about ordering fractions. Gather ideas and, again, ask for comments as you go. Resist the temptation to do too much 'teaching' at this stage. ■ Focus on: – *'How do you know?'* – *'What can you show me to help?'* – Estimating sizes ■ Begin pairs making a teaching poster which explains how to decide if a fraction is bigger or smaller than a 'known' fraction. Allocate different fractions to each pair, differentiating as appropriate.	■ Five minutes before the plenary, ask pairs to rehearse what they might say in explaining their poster. ■ Choose two posters to focus on: – *'What do we like?'* – *'How well do they explain the idea?'* – *'What suggestions could we make?'*

Extensions:

- After refining posters in a subsequent lesson in light of comments from the class, put them up in a public area of the school.

- Leave blank sheets next to them for people to write their own 'comments' on.

- Encourage these people to write about other ways to order fractions and then compare comments with the authors' own ideas.

Year 6

Learning centre-point	Purposeful task	Interactive opportunities – getting started	Interactive opportunities – plenary

Recognise multiples and know some tests of divisibility.	Investigate divisibility and **publish a short paper** on your findings.	■ Play 'guess my number'. (Someone chooses a number <10; teams, in turn, secretly ask about other numbers and are told whether these are multiples of the original number or not; first team to guess the original number wins).
		
		■ Present some two- and three-digit numbers on the board and ask what they are divisible by. Focus on *calculation and classification*:
		  – *'How would you work it out?'*
		  – *'Is there a quicker way?'*
		  – *'Will that always get the answer?'*
		  – *'What patterns are there?'*
		
		■ Use 'talking tokens' (see Chapter 5) to structure the discussion.
		
		■ Focus on 'proof':
		  – *'How sure are you?'*
		  – *'Can you convince someone else that it is true?'*
		  – *'Can you demonstrate it?'*
		
		■ Set groups working on one divisibility test each (extending this to other, more complex ones, as appropriate during the lesson).
		
		■ Use the writing frame provided as a photocopiable on pages 134 and 135 to create a 'mathematics paper' for a maths journal.
			■ Choose one or two groups to present their paper to the rest of the class. Allow preparation time for five minutes prior to the plenary.
			
			■ Encourage the audience to challenge the ideas in the paper, and the authors to defend them.
			
			Or …
			
			■ Hold a poster conference …
			
			■ … papers are left around the edge of the room with a blank A3 sheet next to each one;
			
			■ … groups circulate clockwise from paper to paper;
			
			■ … at each one they read it and leave the authors a comment on the A3 sheet;
			
			■ … finally, authors return to their paper and read the comments.
			
			■ In a final plenary, authors are allowed to defend their papers verbally.

Extensions:

- Publish the papers in a class 'journal' and present it for another class to read.

- Publish it electronically and send it to a class in another school. Ask them to send their papers to you and establish a mathematics dialogue with them.

- Publish the papers on the school website for parents to see.

- Encourage children to ask their own questions at the end of the paper (see writing frame) and to follow these up so that the investigation takes on its own momentum. Pose challenges for each other and/or for other classes.

Summary

- The examples in this chapter aim to provide a picture of how ideas from previous chapters might be implemented in practice.

▶ To what extent are you able to identify ideas discussed in other chapters in the examples? Is it clear to you how they would work?

- The examples are idealised in the sense that not all lessons would be planned like this in practice, though all lessons might have elements of what I have discussed.

▶ What changes could you make in the short term to your own teaching in light of these examples? What would need a longer term solution, and why?

📖 Further reading

Mathematics Teaching is the Journal of the Association of Mathematics Teachers. Issue 181 (December 2002) was a special issue on 'Mathematical Thinking'. The whole issue is well worth looking at.

CHAPTER 7

Starting points for interactive shape and space work

This chapter will ...

■ give an introduction to shape and space, briefly considering what might be the key ideas and principles for teaching it;

■ provide examples and starting points for interactive teaching of shape and space, again modelling different approaches from Chapter 5.

What is shape and space all about?

Clearly, 'shape and space' is about 'shape' and about 'space', but this trivialisation of the topic hides several important points that, I think, are often lost when I see the topic tackled in schools.

The most important point about shape and space work in schools is that children's focus tends to be on 'shapes', rather than on the notion of 'shape'. Perhaps the best example of this distinction is illustrated by the general confusion over squares, oblongs and rectangles. Every year when I teach a shape and space module to undergraduate student teachers I hear people asking what the difference between these words is. Versions of the question include: 'are oblongs just rectangles?'; 'what's the difference between rectangles and squares?'; 'I was told to say rectangles because oblong was a primary school word'; and so on.

Let me first clear up any confusion. *Rectangle* refers to any quadrilateral (four-sided, two dimensional) shape whose corners are all right angled (note that the German for 'right' is 'recht'). You should now be able to see that this *includes* the squares, since they share this property, but also have the property of four equal length sides. This means that squares *are* rectangles. So what about 'oblong'? Well, note that although 'squares are rectangles', the inverse statement 'rectangles are squares' is not always true, since there are many rectangles that are not square – all those where one pair of sides is longer than the other. What we need is a word to describe these 'non-square' rectangles ... and this is what the word 'oblong' does. Figure 7.1 shows this relationship visually. You will see that, in fact, *square* and *oblong* are best thought of as adjectives, not nouns; they describe the kind of rectangle that we are looking at, but they are used so frequently that they revert to nouns more often than not.

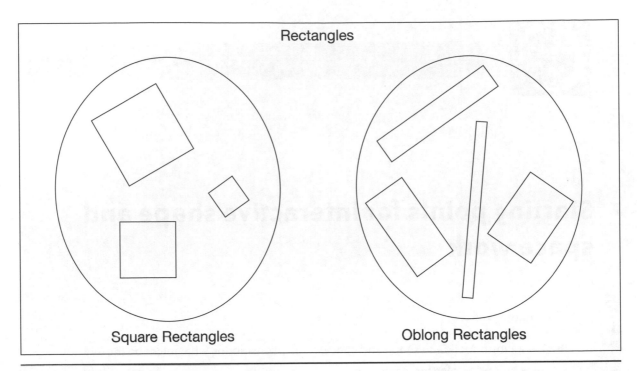

Rectangles

Square Rectangles

Oblong Rectangles

Figure 7.1 Relationships between rectangles

To return now to the distinction between 'shapes' and 'shape', I want to point out that there are lots of 'shapes' which are squares and oblongs, but that each one is named that way because of its 'shape'. Am I teasing you with language? No, the distinction is that each of 'the shapes' is fixed and relates only to that particular one; on the other hand the idea of the 'shape' of squares or oblongs focuses us on the properties that define the whole set of them; spatially what it is about the object that *makes it* a square. This mirrors my claims in Chapter 2 about the nature of maths being essentially to do with ideas. In the case of, say, squares children need to abstract the idea of 'square-ness' from the activity and examples they engage in and then name this idea 'squares'.

Unfortunately, in school, children often do little more than learn the names for 'the shapes' with which they are presented. In other words they tackle things back to front by starting with the names and trying to deduce the properties. It would make better sense to identify the properties, collect all the shapes that fit these properties and then name this set. The name then gets attached to the properties involved – the spatial arrangement that makes the shape what it is – not to isolated examples of them. Of course later, once they know the names and the essential properties that define the set, they will continue to explore further properties.

Where children experience the first of these approaches – naming isolated examples, as they often do – two problems tend to occur. Firstly they cannot understand the *inclusive* nature of shape – that squares can be included *within* rectangles (just as Nick Pratt can be included within 'male' and 'human' etc.). Children who focus on particular shapes, not on the idea of shape, focus on the differences all the time and fail to see the inter-relationships.

Second, and more importantly in the long run, children miss out on all the fun! Simply knowing that a shape is called 'a square' is rather dull; understanding the notion of 'square-ness' and seeing all the relationships and possibilities it holds is much more likely to be of interest. For example, you might like to consider:

■ Is a square a parallelogram?

■ Is a parallelogram a square?

■ Do the diagonals of a square always cross in the middle?

■ For rectangles with a fixed perimeter, the square rectangle always has the biggest area (i.e. all the oblong rectangles with the same perimeter have smaller areas) … how could you demonstrate this?[1]

KEY IDEAS

■ Teaching of shape and space should focus on the spatial relationships that shapes have.

■ We should be helping children to focus on the wider idea of 'shape' and the properties associated with certain sets, not on examples of particular, individual shapes.

■ We should also be focusing on the *implications* of shape properties; what each property implies about the shapes and their relationships to other shapes.

IN YOUR CLASSROOM

■ Do you show children many examples of each shape name so that they do not come to associate the name only with particular versions of it?

■ Do you include highly irregular examples, like this hexagon, as well as the more common ones?

■ Do you draw shapes at different angles so that their bases are not always horizontal?

■ Do you draw out the connections between 2D and 3D shape, showing children that 2D shapes form the boundaries of 3D shapes?

■ Do you use 'near examples' to help children focus on what is and what is not included in each set of shapes? For example, these non-rectangles are all 'near examples':

■ Do you sometimes use made-up names for shapes to help children focus on properties (for example, calling quadrilaterals and pentagons 'fourers' and 'fivers' to focus on sides; or rectangles 'squaries' to focus on corners)?

---

[1] The answers, by the way, are respectively: 'yes, always'; 'only when it's a square one'; 'yes, always'; and 'I'll let you figure it out'.

As I did with number in the previous chapter, I now provide a series of starting points for investigating shape and space across Key Stages 1 and 2, beginning with one example lesson outline. Creating 'purposeful' tasks tends to be easier than for other areas of the mathematics curriculum because of the visual and tactile nature of shape and space. Simply using, holding and manipulating shapes tends to be engaging for children and I have found that they usually need little encouragement to focus intently on what they are doing. On the other hand, this physical manipulation can often be unstructured and children can be too focused on simply 'doing' with little thought given to the implicit shape ideas; the mathematical thinking tends to get lost. My aim, therefore, is to exemplify the shift in emphasis outlined in the first section of this chapter, from looking at shapes towards thinking about properties, patterns and spatial ideas.

Example lesson outline 1: Lines of symmetry (Year 3)

Planning points	Commentary
Learning centre-point: Recognise and sketch more than one line of symmetry.	A typical objective taken from the numeracy curriculum.
Purposeful task: Create a symmetry puzzle book using cut-out paper shapes.	The lesson assumes that the children already have a working knowledge of line symmetry.
Getting started: **Teaching point:** Sit children in a horseshoe with individual whiteboards. Remember to use neutral responses to answers to encourage children to keep thinking creatively.	
Fold a square of paper in half and cut a shape from the folded edge.	
▶ *'Sketch what you think will appear when the paper is unfolded.'*	Encourage children to show their predictions and to reason about why the shape will appear that way. Note that you can use an interactive teaching programme and whiteboard for this but, to me, the physical unfolding of the paper is important.
Fold the paper twice and cut a shape from the folded corner. Again, ask children to sketch what they think will appear.	
Again using two folds, try cutting shapes from different places on the folds of the paper, asking children to predict the outcomes each time	Ask children to describe how the pattern works. Focus on where the folds appear and how these act as lines of symmetry.
Teaching point: Encourage children to close their eyes and to visualise the pattern in their minds.	
Model the unfolding carefully to help children to develop a visual picture of the way it works.	
Teaching point: Resist talking as you unfold the paper, allowing children to concentrate on what is happening visually.	The temptation is to 'tell' the children what is going on yourself. Try, instead, to let *them* do the thinking. Then ask them to describe back to everyone what they were visualising.

▶

Example lesson outline 1: Lines of symmetry (Year 3) continued

Planning points	Commentary
Follow up questions … ▲ *What patterns can you describe to help in predicting the shape?* ▲ *Can you give a rule(s) for working it out?*	Focus on: **Generalisation** and **Procedures** and work as a class to articulate logically the procedures for unfolding the paper, identifying where each 'hole' will end up.
The main task: Provide paper and scissors for children and pair them up. One child makes his or her own pattern by cutting and unfolding secretly before showing his/her partner; the other child then has to try to replicate the pattern by working out how to cut their own piece of folded paper. Take turns.	Encourage children to think about visualising the pattern mentally and using the language of reflection – flip over, reflect, line of symmetry etc.
After a few turns, change to making 'reflection puzzles'. Children create a pattern 'template' – i.e. a folded sheet with bits cut out. They then create several different unfolded patterns, only one of which matches the 'template'. Others have to guess which unfolded pattern originates from the template.	Encourage children to make 'convincing' non-matching patterns. Discuss shapes that might successfully mislead people doing the puzzle. For example, a square cut on a folded edge opens up into an oblong; but putting squares in the false patterns may help to mislead others.
Preparation for the plenary: Five minutes before the plenary, ask children to stick their 'puzzles' onto a large sheet of paper and to prepare for a 'poster conference'. Each pattern on the paper should be labelled with a number or a letter.	
In the plenary: Place all the posters around the room with an A4 sheet and pencils next to each one. Pairs circulate around the posters and write down the letter or number that they think matches the folded 'template'. They can also give reasons for their choice. After all the posters have been visited pairs return to their own to see if others have guessed correctly.	Encourage children to think logically and to visualise how the template will unfold in each puzzle. Though you might want to round off the lesson with a short comment, the work has been done through the independent discussion in pairs and examination of each poster. I would resist too much discussion after the poster conference as it is likely to kill off the enjoyment of the event!

Interaction in practice – Symmetry (Year 3)

Follow up questions …

The teacher has folded the paper left to right and then downwards and cut a square and an equilateral triangle from the top edge. The unfolded pattern will be two oblongs and two 'diamonds' (rhombuses) left and right of the vertical fold line.

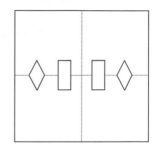

T: What I want you to do is watch as I unfold the paper slowly and picture it in your mind, like playing a video in your head. Try to make your video go just ahead of mine though, so you see it unfolding just before it actually happens. OK … here goes.

[Teacher unfolds the paper slowly.]

T: Right, now, I'm going to do it again and this time I want you to do a commentary to yourself as we go. In your head, imagine describing what is happening to someone else, on a phone maybe. Someone who can't see you. Yes? What would you say to them to describe how each part of the pattern was moving? OK, here goes.

[Teacher again unfolds the paper slowly.]

T: OK, now I want you to talk to your partner and describe to each other what you saw. Try to think about how each part of the pattern moved.

[Children spend a minute talking in pairs.]

T: Right. Now I'm going to make it harder. One person in the pair put your hand up. … OK, you have got to turn round and face the other way. Face the wall over there. Right. Everyone else, you are going to watch me do a new pattern and then you have got to describe it to your partner who is going to try to draw it. Yes, on the whiteboard, that's right.

[Sounds of surprise … groans of general excitement.]

OK, are you ready? No peeping you lot.

[Teacher cuts a new pattern and slowly unfolds it, then hides it away.]

T: OK, turn round the others. Off you go. The one who wasn't looking has got to draw what their partner describes to them. Think about how it unfolded to help you.

Ch1:Can we draw it for them?

T: No, you can only talk … and no pointing and drawing with your fingers either!

[Children talk in their pairs, trying to recreate the pattern.]

T: OK, let's see what's happened. Can you sit round the edge of the carpet? [Children shuffle to the edge.] Right. Here is the pattern I cut out [shows the paper pattern]. How have you done? [General chatter which the teacher lets run … then, interrupting] OK, OK. Listen … listen. I want you to decide who you think got it closest.

Ch1: Marie-Jane.

Ch2: Mine's useless!

Ch3: Jay. His is good.

Ch4: Yeh, his is really close.

[Children continue to comment freely until a general consensus is reached about the best.]

T: Right Jay, your one has got the vote. Can Luke [partner] describe for us what you said to Jay.

Luke: Um … it's hard … I said, like … no, it's hard.

T: OK, well I'll unfold the paper again and you talk out loud. Everyone else, keep quiet as Luke talks, but be ready to make suggestions for different things to say at the end.

Luke: The square starts in the middle of that side and when you unfold it it goes into an oblong.

Ch5: It's like a …

T: [Interrupting] No, stop. You are listening now and then you can say it in a minute. Let Luke finish first.

Luke: Then the oblong goes over to the other side … the same shape … I mean the same place.

T: Ok, thanks Luke, well done. Now, what about others. Any comments?

Ch5: The oblong is like a double square. It's kinda two squares on top of each other.

[Teacher nods but remains silent. Indicates with a gesture for other comments.]

Ch6: They're the same on each side.

T: Can you say any more about that?

Ch6: The same distance [meaning from the centre-fold; again, teacher nods and gestures].

Ch7: The triangle turns into a diamond.

Ch8: Yeh, it kind of gets long.

Ch6: And it goes on the other side again, like the oblong.

T: What do other people think?

Ch9: It is. It's the same over there as over there [indicating on each side of the vertical fold].

T: Several people have said that now. It's the same over here as over here [indicates the two sides again]. What I want to know now is, if I asked for a rule to describe how it unfolds what would you say? I want a rule that tells me where the shapes end up. Talk together first.

[Children talk in pairs for a minute or so. One or two ask for clarification of the task.]

T: OK, what rules would you have?

Ch4:   They're the same size ... the same. Each shape … is the same … you know …

T: No. I don't know yet. Can you explain again.

Ch4:   [Pauses to think.] Both the shapes are the same size.

Ch10: Which shapes?

T: Good question. Which shapes?

Ch4:   The oblongs. They are the same. And the triangles are.

T: OK, thanks. Any other rules?

Ch9:   And they are the same place.

T: How do you mean, same place?

Ch10: He means …

T: [Interrupting] Hold on. Let her finish.

Ch9:   It's the same on this side as that side. The place. This is the same [gets up and indicates distance from central fold to oblong on each side.]

T: Great, OK. Anything else to say?

[The conversation continues for a short while with the teacher continuing to help the children to articulate the ideas behind reflective symmetry.]

It is worth noting how much of the extract above is dominated by the teacher talking, yet it remains interactive in the sense that the children are thinking deeply about how the reflections work. This is a nice example of how interaction can be visual as well as oral – playing up the mental and playing down the oral in 'mental/oral'. It is the visualisation that matters in this task and it is from this that children can then develop the 'rules' for symmetry through discussing these visual images.

Examples of other possible starting points for shape and space

Having presented an example of a lesson outline, the remainder of this chapter provides a series of starting points for investigating shape and space across Key Stages 1 and 2. As in Chapter 6, my aim is to show what is possible – assuming that you will change, adapt, remove and add ideas as you see fit.

Foundation

Learning centre-point	Purposeful task	Interactive opportunities – getting started	Interactive opportunities – plenary
Talk about, recognise and recreate patterns.	**Make jewellery** for a jeweller's shop and **sort it** for display.	■ Create repeating patterns (on the board, with beads on threads etc.) and ask children to discuss 'what comes next'. Make some of the sequences short enough for the pattern not to be fixed so that there are different possibilities open for discussion (e.g. blue-red-blue … could continue … RBRB etc. or repeat as BRB BRB etc.) ■ Look together at examples of real necklaces and bracelets with repeating patterns on them. In pairs, try to explain the patterns verbally. ■ 'Record' the patterns verbally by chanting them: 'blue, red, blue, red …'; 'circle, square, circle, square, square …' etc. Then split the class up so that different groups only say their colour or shape and the groups must work together to chant the pattern. ■ Individually or in pairs, begin to make bracelets or necklaces of their own using string and threading beads, pasta etc.	■ Five minutes before the plenary ask children to practise explaining their pattern to a partner. ■ In a circle, lay out the bracelets and choose individuals to show their patterns. Challenge other children to identify and explain the pattern and see if the maker agrees. ■ Ask children how the jewellery might be sorted in the shop window so that similar items were together. Leave the meaning of 'similar' open so that children can give their ideas about how to sort them.

Extensions:

- Set up a jeweller's shop in the classroom and develop the making and sorting through role-play.

- Create 'rules' for the patterns, verbally at first and then recording them on paper to display in the shop using children's own symbols and drawings.

- Make brooches and pendants out of shiny paper in a variety of different shapes. Include different examples of the 'same' shape, sorting them for the display again (i.e. 'five-sided pendants'; 'curved brooches' etc.).

- Create similar patterns in different contexts (open a whole street of shops!) such as printing patterns for a bedroom wallpaper border, T-shirt designs etc. Ask children to explain their patterns and have an adult scribe this for a display of the items made.

Year 1

Learning centre-point	Purposeful task	Interactive opportunities – getting started	Interactive opportunities – plenary
Describe and classify common 3D shapes.	**Play 'What am I?'** and **make puzzle posters** for a display.	■ Have two sets of identical 3D shapes, one set hidden and one set visible to the children. Put shapes taken from the hidden set one at a time in a 'feely bag'. Pass round the group and challenge children to identify which of the visible shapes it matches. ■ Choose children to feel a new shape and describe it well enough for others to guess which (visible) shape it is the same as. Have them working in pairs and focus them on appropriate language relating to faces, edges and corners. ■ 'Deconstruct' a cuboid cardboard box by cutting it up so that each of the faces is separated. Ask children to talk about their understanding of the shapes and how they fit together to make the cuboid. ■ Select 3D shapes from the original sets and ask children to discuss in pairs what the faces would look like if 'cut up' like the box. ■ Use thick paint (add some PVA glue to it) to create prints of the sides on sugar paper. ■ Set groups of children printing the faces of different 3D shapes.[2]	■ Ask children to practise talking with a partner about the shapes on their printing picture. ■ Encourage questions about the names of different shapes not known by children. Discuss the properties of these shapes and link new (possibly made-up) names to them. ■ Choose some children to show their printing pictures and challenge others to decide which 3D shape it came from based on the prints of the faces. Receive different answers and then ask children to justify their decisions.

[2] Clearly, this will best be done one group at a time whilst the other children work on another task!

Extensions:

- Display the pictures and invite another class into the room to see if they can recognise the original shape. Encourage your children to explain how the pictures work.

- Investigate the shadows that 3D shapes cast when placed on an OHP. Use a cardboard screen round the OHP to hide the shape and see if children can guess what it is as you rotate it onto different surfaces.

- Make a 'shape museum' using packaging from home. Each 'artefact' (shape) must have a label describing some of its key features (properties).

Year 2

Learning centre-point	Purposeful task	Interactive opportunities – getting started	Interactive opportunities – plenary
Make and describe common 2D shapes.	Make **shape pictures** identifying new shapes within them.	■ Use a large cardboard square and draw round it on the board. Then move the square slightly and draw round it again.[3] Discuss the shapes created by the intersection and the remaining regions of the original squares. ■ Repeat this operation creating different intersections each time and discuss the resulting sets of shapes. ■ Challenge children, discussing in small groups, how to create: triangles of different sorts; rectangles of different sorts; as many rectangles/triangles as possible; a five-sided shape; an eight-sided shape etc. Providing two squares of coloured acetate (from a stage lighting shop) or tracing paper will help children to experiment. ■ Let children work individually either on a computer or with plastic shapes to draw around on a sheet of A3 paper. Encourage them to explore the different shapes that can be made.	■ Five minutes before the plenary, introduce the idea of categorising each pattern according to the sides of the shapes created. For example, the two illustrations on the left might be 'two sixers and a fourer' (because a square and two irregular hexagons are created) and 'an eighter, and eight threers' (octagon and eight triangles). ■ Ask children to work out what their examples would be and to bring their thinking to the plenary. ■ During the plenary create a list of different categories. Group them so that, say, all the ones involving 'fourers' are together. Look for 'missing' shapes or new versions together ('has anyone found a fiver … a different fourer?').

[3] Instead of drawing with a marker pen, use Microsoft Word's drawing facility to create two squares. Select the shapes one at a time with a right click on the mouse to get a pop-up menu and choose the 'format autoshape' option. 'Fill' them in two different colours and make them 50% 'transparent'. When placed over each other, the intersection is seen as a mix of the two colours. One or both squares can then be rotated and translated on an interactive whiteboard.

Extensions:

■ Use different starting shapes.

■ Use more than two shapes to create more complex patterns.

■ Set up an 'investigation zone' in the classroom with equipment (a computer, coloured acetates or simply plastic shapes, pencils and paper) for children to experiment with during free time.

Year 3

Learning centre-point	Purposeful task	Interactive opportunities – getting started	Interactive opportunities – plenary
Make and describe 2D shapes and sort them according to their properties.	**Make simple shape sets** by cutting polygons.	■ Begin by displaying examples of a number of common polygons made from paper. Make the examples different and include some unusual ones (e.g. a very long thin triangle). ■ Ask children to work in pairs and to choose one secretly and plan how they might describe it. ■ Choose pairs to describe their choice out loud for others to try to identify (a harder version is for others to have to ask yes/no questions to identify it). ■ Select a **rectangle** and cut it (with a straight cut) into two new polygons. Ask children for comments about what they see and think. ■ Cut **one** of the new polygons again, discussing the two new shapes that are created. Focus on properties, then link a shape name to them. ■ Begin again with a new rectangle. This time cut it differently so that a different set of three shapes is created. ■ Provide lots of paper rectangles and challenge children to make two cuts of their own like this to create some specific sets of three shapes – start by making three rectangles; three triangles; one each of triangle, quadrilateral and pentagon etc.	■ Five minutes before the plenary, ask children to choose one of their sets of polygons to focus on and to get ready to describe it to others in terms of sides and angles. ■ Begin to group the sets of shapes according to children's descriptions of their properties. Focus on number of sides and types of angles. ■ If appropriate, discuss and agree what it means for two shapes to be 'different'. ■ Discuss labels that might be given to each set to describe its contents and build up to a simple display. Include spare rectangles and scissors as part of this and encourage children to return to it in spare moments to find new examples.

Year 3 continued

Learning centre-point	Purposeful task	Interactive opportunities – getting started	Interactive opportunities – plenary
		■ Then challenge them to create as many *different* sets of three polygons as possible. Leave the meaning of 'different' in this context vague and open to discussion. Are two rectangles of varying size different (because of their size) or the same (because they are both rectangles)? ■ Tip: get children to glue their three shapes onto sugar paper each time so they don't get muddled up.	

Extensions:

■ Start with a shape other than a rectangle.

■ Allow a third cut to make four polygons and look at the new sets you can make.

■ Challenge each other to put the pieces back together again to recreate the original starting shape.

■ Use the polygons created as simple *tangram* pieces and investigate new shapes that can be made with them.

■ Encourage children to create their own 'challenges' for others and display these (for example: 'What is the shape with the most sides that you can make?'; 'Can you make at least two squares?' etc.).

Year 4

Learning centre-point	Purposeful task	Interactive opportunities – getting started	Interactive opportunities – plenary
Make 2D shapes with increasing accuracy.	Play 'make me draw it' and design a poster explaining the properties of 2D shapes. Hold a poster conference.	■ Challenge the children to *force* you to draw a chosen 2D shape. Pairs take it in turn to give instructions which you must follow whilst trying to *avoid* drawing the shape. For example, if children start the instructions for a square by telling you to 'draw a line', you might draw a curved line. ■ Encourage children to talk together about these instructions. (Note how the game demands clarity about the key spatial features of the shape.) Take opportunities, as they arise, to discuss 'what is meant by …?'. ■ Split the class into two groups and play again with one group giving instructions and the other group trying to avoid drawing the shape. Encourage clarity in what is being said. ■ Set children working in fours with two pairs playing against each other. ■ After ten minutes change the task so that each group must produce a poster explaining the key properties of one or more of the shapes they have been playing with. The poster must explain exactly how to generate the shape.	■ Run a poster conference. Each group places their poster around the edge of the room. Blank A4 sheets are left next to them. Each group circulates around the room looking at the posters and leaving a comment on the A4 sheet. ■ Encourage comments to identify both clear thinking and possible challenges to the instructions for drawing the shape(s). ■ Groups return to their posters to read comments. Then discuss alterations that might be made to their posters in light of any challenges.

Extensions:

- Extend the complexity of the shapes. Circles are particularly interesting. Note that they appear difficult to define, but can easily be forced by giving the following instructions: draw a dot; place the pen anywhere other than on the dot; draw a curve, always remaining an equal distance from the dot and continue until you reach your starting point again.

- Use the posters to write concise definitions of each shape and publish these in a class shape and space 'dictionary'.

- Use LOGO or a floor robot and work out simple programmable instructions to draw the shapes.

- Take long lengths of elastic and stitch the ends together to make a large loop. Challenge groups to stretch the elastic into different shapes by holding it and moving in different ways.

Year 5

Learning centre-point	Purposeful task	Interactive opportunities – getting started	Interactive opportunities – plenary

Constructing 3D models with increasing accuracy.	Work with **shape sets** to build 3D models.
	
	Explore **all possible outcomes.**
		■ Use a 3D building material such as 'Polydron', 'Clixi' or 'MATs.'[4]
		
		■ Provide everyone with just eight 'pieces' of any mix of shapes and ask them to build a 3D solid using some or all of them. Once everyone has made their shape, stand them up and ask them to find similarities between shapes and to make groups accordingly.
		
		■ Start again, rebuilding the shapes. Challenge children to try to build a shape with unusual properties so that they are standing on their own when they form groups.
		
		■ Provide groups with a new 'shape set' and challenge them to find all the possible 3D shapes that can be made from it. Try a limited number of:
		  – triangles and squares only
		  – hexagons and triangles only
		  – hexagons and squares only
		  – octagons and triangles only
			■ Prior to the plenary focus children on the faces, edges and vertices of their shape.
			
			■ Use these ideas to talk about the shapes and to classify them in the plenary.
			
			■ Discuss whether or not the children have found them all in each case.

[4] MATs are cardboard shapes produced by the Association of Teachers of Mathematics. They can be laid out on tables for 2D work or stuck together with glue to make 3D solids.

Extensions:

- Explore all the nets that can be unfolded from each shape.

- Use 'sets' of pipe-cleaners and straws (or a commercially available alternative) to build skeletal models instead of solids. (Note that skeletal models focus children's attention on edges and vertices, rather than faces.)

- Allow children to use just one regular 2D shape, but as many as they like. This will provide an opportunity to find the five regular solids (triangles lead to the tetrahedron, octahedron and icosahedron, squares to the cube and pentagons to the dodecahedron).

Year 6

Learning centre-point	Purposeful task	Interactive opportunities – getting started	Interactive opportunities – plenary
Know properties of common 2D shapes	**Hold a debate** about controversial shape properties.	■ Draw a set of images like those shown here. Discuss 'what is happening to the kite'. ■ Ask children to discuss in pairs what they think will happen next to it. (Note: it will momentarily become a triangle before becoming a deltoid (arrowhead).) ■ What about stretching it the other way? ■ Is it always a kite, or does it turn into other things? Use this question to discuss how children are defining the idea of 'kite'.[5] Note how the idea of 'kite' is less certain than it might have been before and needs arguing about, agreeing and defining. ■ Encourage children to deliberately create arguments 'for and against' and try, as a class, to 'attack' the arguments by reasoning and finding counter examples. ■ Split the class into two groups and ask them to discuss one of the following statements (or make up your own). Provide appropriate equipment to help children model the ideas. One group must argue *for* the statement and the other *against* it … – Equilateral triangles are just special cases of isosceles triangles. – Rectangles are special parallelograms.[6] – Diagonals can never be vertical or horizontal.[7] – The order of rotational symmetry is always the same as the number of sides for 2D shapes.[8] – 3D shapes don't have diagonals.[9] – Four cubes can be glued together in only six different ways.[10]	■ Allow 20–30 minutes for the discussion. ■ Provide 'talking tokens' in two different colours: one for statements; one for questions. ■ Children give up a token of the appropriate colour each time they speak. ■ Take the statements in turn and debate their validity. By controlling the number of tokens you can encourage all children to speak and no one child to dominate.

[5] Note that some dictionaries are happy to include deltoids as kites (inverted kites, if you like) whilst others define kites to have all their angles non-reflex (i.e. <180).

[6] Yes – since parallelograms are defined as being quadrilaterals with two pairs of parallel sides. Rectangles are simply a special case of the parallelogram where all four corners are right angles (and note that squares are special cases of rectangles – and hence of parallelograms too – where all sides are also the same length).

[7] Clearly they can (imagine a square standing on one corner), but this statement encourages children to distinguish between the word 'diagonal' in general and 'the diagonal(s)' of a shape.

[8] True for *regular* shapes, but not for all 2D shapes in general.

[9] Diagonals in 3D shapes are generally only considered to be those that connect vertices *not* in the same face. In other words, diagonals on the faces do not count and all diagonals must pass through points 'inside' the shape. A cube, for example, therefore has four digonals.

[10] There are six different ways to arrange four cubes where 'different' means that rotations and reflections are considered to be 'the same' as each other. If they are considered as 'different' then the number of solutions increases.

Extensions:

■ Play 'Call My Bluff' with statements that the children have invented. For each statement children create an accurate answer and two plausible, inaccurate ones and then others must guess which is which.

■ Ask children to write down their arguments, focusing on clarity and accuracy. Then email these to children at another school for them to respond to … and receive similar statements from them to puzzle over.

Summary

- Shape and space work should be about the sense of shape, not just about particular shapes that appear regularly, and their names. Names are important but properties are the key thing and names should be linked to these.

▶ How does the claim above relate to your view of shape and space? Do you tend to focus on names or on properties? Are you able to make connections between shapes and understand their properties?

- Encouraging children to sort, construct and take apart shapes and to discuss what they can see will help children to focus on properties.

▶ What kinds of tasks have you given children in the past for shape and space? Have these encouraged children to see new properties and to think creatively and logically about the relationships between shapes?

📖 Further reading

Johnston-Wilder, S. and Mason, J. (2005) *Developing Thinking in Geometry*. London: Paul Chapman.
Ebbutt, S. and Mosley, F. (1996) *Exploring Shape and Space*. London: BEAM.

CHAPTER 8

Developing your interactive teaching

This chapter will ...

■ review the key ideas from previous chapters in order to summarise the themes from the book and introduce assessment of children's mathematical work;

■ suggest ways to audit your teaching of mathematics, or that of colleagues in your school;

■ provide suggestions for changing practice and starting points for more extended continuing professional development.

Identifying potential areas for change

I began this book by saying that the ideas I was suggesting were, in some ways, aspirational. I do not mean that they are not possible, nor that they are all difficult to implement. They do, however, challenge some of the existing ways of doing things – approaches that seem well embedded in school practices and which have the weight of government authority behind them in many cases. In this sense, to do the things I have suggested and, more importantly, to do them with the right kind of intent, you must be willing to both identify the possibilities for change in the classroom and take the risk of trying new ideas. This chapter aims to help you to make these changes – on an individual level and/or as a school or department.

The earlier chapters are reviewed in turn and some of the key ideas are revisited from each one. These are then developed in terms of ways in which you might:

■ audit your needs (or the needs of your school);

■ make some short term changes to your practice;

■ plan to investigate the situation more fully through your own classroom-based research.

In suggesting changes I make no attempt to tell you what to think. That kind of approach has been shown to have only a very superficial effect on practice – and has prompted the writing of this book. Instead, I offer ideas and leave it to your own professional judgement to take them at face value or to adapt them to your own needs. You should, of course, plan your own ideas too as you see fit.

Key theme 1 – mathematical experiences

In Chapter 2 I introduced the idea that the experiences children have in mathematics affect not the amount of mathematical knowledge they develop but the form of that knowledge itself.

KEY IDEAS REVISITED

- *How* we teach directly affects not just children's attitudes but also the *form* of knowledge that they develop.

- Children who learn in a climate of enquiry and who engage in problem solving regularly, tend to develop knowledge that is more flexible and can be put to use more readily.

In addition to these key ideas, Chapter 2 introduced the triangular relationship between *doing maths, knowing maths* and *using maths*.

Audit 1 – your children's mathematical diet

Use the checklist below to audit the mathematical experiences provided for your children. Each question is followed by statements at two ends of a spectrum. You might consider where you lie on this spectrum and whether this is where you would *like* to be.

Key question: To what extent are mathematical ideas *developed through* engagement in problem solving? …	
… most of children's maths is centred on solving problems or at least presented in a 'problematic context'.	… mathematical ideas are taught independently and in isolation and problem solving is done as a separate topic.
… problem solving involves a range of different kinds of problem including those within the real world and within maths itself.	… problem solving always relates only to word problems.
… problem solving is seen as an ongoing stance towards teaching – part of a conjecturing atmosphere – rather than something that is done on particular days.	… problem solving is planned and carried out on a regular, but infrequent, basis as a particular activity.
… opportunities are taken for using mathematics as a means of solving problems in other areas of the curriculum.	… mathematical work only takes place in 'mathematics' lessons.
… children are encouraged to raise and investigate their own questions about their mathematical work.	… all children's work is set and directed by the teacher.

Key question:	To what extent are *mathematical processes* part of ongoing teaching and learning? …
… questions and tasks encourage children to reason and communicate about mathematics all the time.	← → … questions and tasks are there to be completed and little emphasis is placed on *how* this is done.
… generalising, conjecturing and proof/ justification are firmly embedded in children's activity.	← → … children are rarely required to generalise, make conjectures and justify their thinking about things.
… children get plenty of opportunity to communicate their mathematical thinking to a range of audiences and through a range of formats (speaking, posters, diaries etc.).	← → … all mathematical work is recorded in exercise books for the benefit of the teacher.
… children get chances to engage in extended mathematical activities, sometimes going on over several lessons.	← → … mathematical activity takes place in single lessons and children are always expected to complete the task within this time.

Short term suggestions

The following list reviews ideas presented elsewhere in the book that you might want to try in the short term in relation to the audit above. Note that these should be seen as experimental – ideas to try out and explore – not as quick fix solutions to a situation. As I have tried to convey throughout this book, all classrooms create their own context and though there may be useful advice for all teachers, significant change has to be done through ownership on your part. It is your commitment to the process of change that matters as much as the change itself. More extended, long term suggestions for classroom-based research follow in the next section, but in the short term:

▶ Rethink your lesson objectives and phrase them as open questions.

▶ Look at the *verbs* you use in your lesson objectives. Instead of 'learn that …' try using:

– investigate …

– explore …

– experiment with …

– justify why/how…

– practise …

– develop ways to …

Think up new verbs to focus on different mathematical processes.

▶ Model the raising of questions as children work and record these for further exploration. End lessons by asking children to suggest further work that could be undertaken in the same area.

▶ Plan to use mathematics to solve problems in other curriculum areas.

▶ Plan explicitly to ask process-based questions during your teaching. Refer back to the list in 'asking and responding to questions' in Chapter 5.

▶ Try out some new ways of recording mathematical work. Provide children with a degree of choice over this.

▶ Plan work that lasts over more than one lesson. Start with an open question and encourage children to ask their own subsidiary questions to follow-up. (Note that they will find this difficult at first if they have not previously been asked to do it.)

Classroom-based research

Whilst the list above might help you to make immediate changes, exploring the effect of these in the longer term will require a more extended and systematic approach. It is beyond the scope of this book to discuss in detail how to go about practitioner-based research projects of this sort, but further reading is suggested at the end of the chapter for this. You might also seek support from a local higher education institution and undertake this kind of research as part of the school's, or your own, ongoing continuing professional development programme.

As a starting point for your own research, you might try one or more of the following ideas.

▶ Make some kind of change to your practice, starting with a small, simple thing that you are confident about trying. As you make the change, keep a (brief) reflective log to help you understand the effects these changes are having.

▶ If you work as part of a team, do this together and discuss it as and when you can.

▶ Build this reflective process into your performance management cycle by making it a target for your professional development and the focus of any observations undertaken by colleagues.

▶ Create time to talk to your children about their experiences. Ask them how they would teach the class and what it feels like to be a pupil in it. Even better, get a trusted colleague to do this for you.

▶ Ask a trusted colleague to teach your class whilst you teach theirs and to report back to you. They are likely to pick up the norms and expectations in your class and may be able to shed new light on what you do.

▶ Use a video and record your teaching to look back on later. (Have chocolate or a glass of wine to hand and lock the door – it may be an uncomfortable experience at first!)

▶ Keep a diary of classroom events which illustrate particular issues in order to help you to focus on them. For example, record occasions where children said unexpected things, or questions that worked particularly well. Note your response each time and reflect on how effective it was.

► If you keep children's work as part of a portfolio, extend the range of criteria you work with. Try to find pieces that reflect things such as: good communication; effective reasoning; creative solutions to problems etc.

► Read *Mathematics in School* and *Mathematics Teaching*, the journals of the Mathematical Association and the Association of Teachers of Mathematics respectively (see Further Reading). These contain lots of articles based on classroom research and will help to inform and frame questions about your own classroom. Why not try writing up your work for one of these too?

► Start your own maths 'blog'. Raise some questions and see what responses you get!

Finally, be aware that one danger of examining what you do more closely than normal is that things may feel worse before they get better. Being active in thinking about what you are doing is likely to highlight things you want to change. Note that you have always done these things … you are now just more aware of them! Noticing them is the first, uncomfortable but necessary, step to being able to change them.

Starting points

The ideas above should help you to find a way to begin examining your maths teaching. In order to decide what to focus on, I have listed questions (below) which should act as a starting point for this investigation. Obviously you cannot tackle them all, so choose one or two that interest you most.

► What do my children think 'maths' and 'maths work' is all about?

► If they do not see it as a process of investigation and exploration, how can I encourage this more?

► What sorts of problem solving do I use in my maths teaching and what do children think about this?

► How can I extend the range of problems I use and what constrains me in this respect?

► How can I create a more effective 'conjecturing atmosphere' in my classroom?

► How can I develop children's ability to ask their own mathematical questions as part of their work?

► What mathematical processes does my teaching encourage children to develop?

► How can I extend the range of these?

► What happens to children's attitudes towards maths when they do less recording in books?

► How do other forms of recording change their approach to the subject, if at all?

▶ How long are children prepared to work on a task I set them before they give up and expect me to help them?

▶ How can I extend this time?

Key theme 2 – mathematical communication

In Chapter 3 I introduced the idea that understanding was relative to both time and place and was never complete. Moreover, it makes little sense to talk about understanding as if it were 'owned' by an individual, since what one understands is also relative to the other people with whom you are communicating.

KEY IDEAS REVISITED

■ We need to try to create classroom tasks in which communication about maths is *part of* the task, not incidental to it.

■ Classroom talk needs to be structured enough to help children make sense; this is different to 'social' talk.

■ Ideally, children (and their teachers) should begin to see understanding as something that is never completed and as shared between people (we understand more together when we communicate about it).

Audit 2 – the talk in your classroom

Key question: How is your classroom set up for talking? …	
… there is a lot of talk going on all the time in the classroom.	… most of the mathematical work children do is undertaken in silence.
… children are organised in groups *in order* to talk more effectively.	… children are organised in order to work independently.
… the tasks set for children involve talking as an integral part of their completion.	… tasks set for children give little thought to talk, which is undertaken only on an *ad hoc* basis.
… whole class teaching is organised and managed to encourage a wide range of participation.	… participation is limited to only a few individuals who tend to dominate.

Key question: What do you, and your children, see talk as being *for*? ...	
... talking is seen as a way of making sense of ideas.	←→ ... talking is seen as 'telling', with the focus on transmission from one person to another.
... talking is seen as a joint process so that people 'make sense' together. Listening is active and seen as transformative.	←→ ... talking is seen largely as a means of identifying important points for others to remember.
Key question: What expectations do you hold about the *way* children talk in your classroom? ...	
... there are different forms of talk with different purposes. Talking for learning is seen as different to social talk.	←→ ... all talking is seen as the same. Children can talk in any way they like at any time.
... children are expected to talk publicly with some clarity and to develop this ability through regular practice as part of their work in mathematics.	←→ ... all kinds of talk are acceptable and children who are finding it hard are 'rescued' so that they never learn to develop it.

Short term suggestions

► Plan tasks which require talking together for their completion.

► Make clear to children that talking is part of the task, and how it is so; try not to let talk only be incidental and *ad hoc*.

► Extend the time that you wait for answers to your own questions by counting to three, then gradually to five, then seven etc.

► Use the suggestions in Chapter 5 to avoid 'killing off' discussion through revealing the right answer too quickly.

► Similarly, use the suggestions for 'involving everyone' to extend the range of responses both in terms of who is speaking and what is said.

► Talk about talk with children! Engender an atmosphere of 'making sense together' and of talk as 'work' (see Chapters 4 and 5).

► Hold back from helping children too much when they are trying to articulate their ideas. Give them time to form their responses and develop the expectation that these should be as articulate as possible.

► Provide more opportunities for children to rehearse their responses to questions with another child before speaking to the whole class.

Starting points for classroom-based research

► What do children in my class think talking is for?

► To what extent am I 'judge and jury' (see Chapter 4) of what people should think and say in my classroom?

▶ What might I want to change in this respect and how might I do this?

▶ What proportion of whole class talk is the teacher's; what proportion is the children's?

▶ What might be the pros and cons of changing this proportion and how can I do so?

▶ How can I develop tasks that involve talking as part of their purpose?

▶ What effect does changing children's talking patterns have on their attainment in maths?

▶ What about the effect on their disposition towards the subject?

▶ What expectations do I have of classroom talk?

▶ How can I help children develop their talk so that they speak more clearly and use it more effectively for thinking together?

Key theme 3 – classroom discourses

In Chapter 4 I introduced the notion of discourses and the idea that there are likely to be at least two different discourses operating simultaneously in the classroom – a discourse relating to classroom management and a discourse relating to mathematics.

KEY IDEAS REVISITED

■ Teachers' interactions with children involve a balance between the ongoing mathematical and classroom discourses.

■ This balance is affected by many things, including the ways in which teachers:

  ■ ask questions;

  ■ respond to and appropriate children's ideas;

  ■ model and demonstrate;

  ■ evaluate and correct responses;

  ■ facilitate discussion and listen carefully.

■ The most effective interaction is likely to happen when children's focus is more explicitly on the mathematical discourse with the classroom discourse being implicit and in the background.

Audit 3 – your classroom discourse(s)

Key question: How strong is each discourse in your classroom? ...		
… children are free to think mathematically and the focus is on the *accuracy* of the mathematics.	←→	… children focus on what is 'right/wrong' and are tied implicitly to what the teacher wants to hear.
… many questions are open and children have the chance to think mathematically in answering them.	←→	… most questions are looking for a particular answer and tend to follow the initiation-response-feedback pattern.
… non-conforming or inaccurate answers are seen as creative and interesting; time is spent following them up.	←→	… non-conforming or inaccurate answers are seen as wrong and are rejected as 'bad'.
… children are keen to talk about what they are thinking mathematically and to show how they do things.	←→	… children are reluctant to think out loud and want to keep their working to themselves.
Key question: How do you manage classroom interactions? ...		
… a range of questions is used, modelling and encouraging different mathematical processes.	←→	… most questions ask for recall of knowledge.
… explanations, demonstrations and modelling are used appropriately to show children new ideas. Questions are used genuinely to find out what people think.	←→	… questions are used all the time even when particular answers are sought.
… children's responses are listened to carefully; a serious attempt is made to understand them and to develop ideas from them.	←→	… children's answers are often largely ignored and glossed over if they are not immediately intelligible.
… the accuracy of answers is not immediately revealed, helping children to think more extensively about their responses.	←→	… responses are judged immediately as right/wrong and children switch off as soon as they know the answer.
… children's ideas are used to develop new ideas where possible.	←→	… children's answers are appropriated to fulfil the teacher's own agenda, regardless of what is said.
… the focus is on the accuracy of the mathematics, not on right/wrong.	←→	… the focus is on right/wrong. Wrong answers are addressed in depth; right ones are glossed over.

Short term suggestions

The whole of Chapter 5 was focused on suggestions for changing practice in respect of the points in the audit above. I recommend that you revisit the chapter and review the ideas.

Starting points for classroom-based research

▶ What would children say about the way in which my classroom operates?

▶ To what extent am I aware of the ways in which I respond to children's contributions in my class?

▶ How could I develop this awareness, perhaps by recording my teaching and watching/listening carefully to what I do, or through peer observation?

▶ How engaged are my children in thinking mathematically?

▶ What is the *range* of this thinking? What do they do well and what not so well?

▶ What could I do to develop this range?

▶ How effectively do I listen to children and use their responses in my teaching?

▶ How could I do this more effectively?

Key theme 4 – assessing children's mathematical work

The major aim of this book has been to offer the reader a more sophisticated and useful picture of teaching and learning in maths than the one portrayed by government initiatives. In particular I have tried to focus on the *intent* behind teaching practices and a wider, richer view of what mathematics entails. Similarly, I have tried to portray maths as a subject which is best learnt together through cooperative interaction and have suggested that the notion of individual understanding is problematic. A child's 'understanding' of the subject is dependent on a number of factors relating to the social context (who they are working with, why they are doing it, how they are being asked etc.). As I suggested in Chapter 3, understanding is also a temporary state, constantly in motion, not a fixed attribute of the child. In essence then, one cannot separate *what* children learn from *how* they learn it and *how* they are asked about it. One important aspect of this is that the particular situation of a test, or a task specifically designed to assess 'an idea', will not show us the same thing as assessment undertaken during everyday classroom practice. This is not to say that such tests are not useful … just that they do not tell the same story because of the change in the context for learning.

Given these points, it would be a shame if we did not give some thought to how we might assess the subject from this perspective. You might immediately ask whether it has become so complex that it is impossible to make any sort of assessment at all. I would suggest that the problem here is to do with what we hope to achieve through assessment. If the idea is to label a fixed state of the child (to say they are 'this good' at maths) then this is indeed impossible – though we may have to try anyway because of the demands of the assessment system. I am more interested though in the question: 'what can we say about the child that is useful to us in teaching him or her?' – assessment for learning.

Having made things more complex, I now want to be more pragmatic in two distinct ways. First, though we can never capture all the subtleties of what it might mean to be an expert mathematician, we can at least be more aware of the *range of things that this might involve*. Not only is this a good idea because it helps to remind us, and children, what the subject is really about, but it is also more inclusive since it provides a better opportunity for children to be good at it. Note that all assessment involves a value judgement of some sort. For example, if we value 'pace' then children who need more time are suddenly labelled as 'not so good' at the subject, when they might equally well be labelled as 'successfully' thoughtful and curious.

PRACTICAL EXAMPLE

At parents' evening the other day my wife and I were told that our oldest daughter rarely offered anything orally when the class worked on the carpet. In this respect the teacher implied that she 'needed to do better' – albeit within the context of a generally positive report. When we asked her about this the next day she told us:

'He always goes so quickly though dad. I'm still thinking about it and it's already been done. I can do it; just not so quickly like that.'

▶ Would you say that my daughter has a problem or not? If so, whose problem is it?

The second way of being pragmatic about assessment is to offer a checklist of the contextual issues you might want to consider as you assess children's achievements and attainment. This helps to answer the question: 'will things always appear this way?'

These two approaches to assessment are tackled through an audit of the range and context of assessment in the following section.

Audit 4 – the range and context of mathematical achievement

Koshy offers a nice model of mathematical 'key concepts' (Figure 8.1, p. 124) which helps to remind us of both aspects of the mathematics itself (the outer ring) and of our interaction with, and dispositions towards, these (the inner ring).

The labels in this model refer to the following ideas:

- *Generalisation* – making general statements of 'what is happening', seeing patterns and creating rules

- *Proof* – justifying why and how something is the case

- *Isomorphism* – recognising mathematics learnt in one context in other contexts and being able to make this transfer oneself

- *Algorithm* – developing procedures for carrying out mathematical tasks and operations

- *Conjecture* – making and testing statements about what might happen

- *Curiosity* – being interested and attentive and wanting to find out more

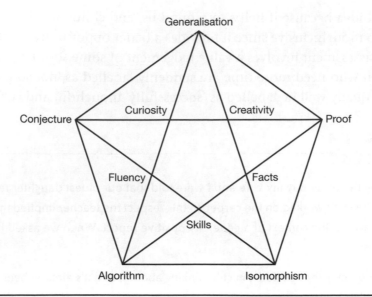

Figure 8.1 Mathematical key concepts (Koshy, 2001, p. 33. Permission granted by David Fulton Publishers Ltd, part of the Grenada Learning Group.)

- *Creativity* – creating new ideas and seeing possibilities that others have not spotted

- *Facts* – knowing key pieces of information and being able to use these in their work

- *Skills* – being able to carry out practical tasks and procedures

- *Fluency* – using maths efficiently and smoothly

These ideas offer us a richer and more holistic view of the subject than the normal state of affairs, where the focus is usually on children's ability to memorise key information and ideas and to use these in a limited range of contexts.

Key question: What is valued in children's mathematical work? ...		
... assessment approaches take account of the full range of ideas in the model above.	←→	... assessment focuses on memory of key ideas and facts.
... there are multiple ways of being successful in mathematics.	←→	... success is only related to accuracy and speed.
... personal dispositions (inner ring) are considered as important as mathematical understandings (outer ring).	←→	... assessment only focuses on mathematical understandings.
... oral work is used alongside written work in making judgements about children's mathematics.	←→	... written work is the only evidence used in making judgements.

Key question: What account is taken of the task undertaken by children in assessing work in mathematics? ...	
... children are assessed through their ongoing classroom mathematics as well as through specifically designed tasks and tests. ◄—►	... mathematics is only assessed through specifically designed tasks and tests.
... assessment opportunities include the chance to work in a range of contexts, including real life problem solving, word problems, investigative activities, recall/practice tasks etc. ◄—►	... assessment is all done through specifically designed worksheets.
... assessment tasks are sufficiently open-ended for children to show the full range of their capability. ◄—►	... assessment is largely focused on particular ideas addressed through closed questions.
Key question: What account is taken of the social context in assessing work in mathematics? ...	
... judgements are made with children working in a range of different organisational modes (individually, in groups, as a class etc.). ◄—►	... all assessment is of individual work.
... teachers are aware that assessment is subjective and that even 'individual' work is dependent on the underlying expectations, appearing different as the context changes. ◄—►	... assessment is seen as entirely objective, independent of the situation within which it is undertaken.
... teachers are aware that understanding is never an attribute of an individual and is always a function of the relationship between people (and the tasks they create). ◄—►	... understanding is seen as an essential attribute of the child independent of anything else.

Short term suggestions

▶ Use the assessment grid provided as a photocopiable on pages 136 an 137 to ensure you consider all the aspects of mathematical work suggested by Koshy in Figure 8.1, p. 124.

▶ Pick a child who you feel is less successful at maths and deliberately explore whether they can be made to appear more successful by widening your definition of 'success'. Similarly, explore whether 'successful' children might appear less so with different criteria in mind.

▶ Discuss what it means to be successful in maths with children and seek their views on this. Talk about what a successful mathematician might *do*, as well as what they might *know*.

▶ Ask children what advice they would give about maths to a new child joining the class. This may help to reveal the things that children value in your classroom.

▶ Provide a range of tasks that make use of the same mathematical idea in different ways and compare the way children respond to each one.

▶ Actively consider the effects of context by asking yourself what is likely to feel important from the child's point of view (being seen to be accurate, playing safe etc.).

▶ Ensure that assessment tasks have sufficient open-endedness to allow children to show what they can really do. Include open questions as well as more closed ones.

▶ Ask children to assess each other, perhaps using some of the headings in the photocopiable assessment grids. Discuss what it would look like to get better at each aspect.

Starting points for classroom-based research

▶ What aspects of children's mathematics do I currently value and why?

▶ To what extent does this match the children's expectations?

▶ What is the effect of these values on the assessment I make and who does it advantage/disadvantage?

▶ How might changing what I value in my teaching alter the apparent attainment of the children in my class?

▶ To what extent is this realistic in the school environment within which I work?

▶ To what extent is the apparent attainment/achievement of children limited or afforded by the tasks that I provide?

▶ How can I alter the tasks I use to develop a more inclusive and holistic approach to assessing mathematics?

▶ What does it mean in practice if understanding is shared between people in a group? What implications does this have for my assessment?

▶ What are the connections between *what* and *how* I assess mathematics and the way in which children engage in maths in my classroom?

▶ Can I help children to learn more effectively by changing my assessment procedures (see the 'Assessment for Learning' materials in the Further Reading section below).

Conclusion

The spotlight on assessment that brings this chapter to a close is apposite because it refocuses us on learning and its relationship with teaching. This association, and particularly the idea that it is the subtle intent behind action that matters most, has been at the centre of the book.

I began with three premises that I claimed underpinned the ideas I wanted to write about. The first was that teaching should be an essentially straightforward affair in that it is essentially about people communicating with each other – a natural human endeavour. We have seen that this statement belies the intricacies of the communicative process though and, in particular, that communication is strongly influenced by the discourses of the classroom. I hope that this idea of discourse has been useful to you in understanding the context you work in more clearly.

My second premise was that effective learning is essentially related to thinking more deeply about things. Again, this is more complex in practice than I make it sound, but I hope that the practical ideas I have offered along the way, and the manner in which I have tried to help you to develop a related theoretical perspective on them, have been supportive in terms of your own teaching. Indeed, this connection between theory and practice formed the basis of my third premise.

In hindsight I should have added a fourth premise: that *learning and teaching should, above all, be enjoyable*. 'Fun', would not be the right word – it can be too difficult and demanding for that much of the time; but enjoyable, certainly. If I have one criticism of the current school system it would be that it all seems very pressured. Since teaching and learning are fundamentally about relationships then surely these should be enjoyable, friendly, relaxed and amusing ones – the kind that we like in our non-working relationships. Perhaps 'less' might be 'more' if we stood back and looked more carefully; took more time and gave more space for thinking; rejected the idea of right and wrong and replaced it with more or less accurate; viewed 'understanding' as 'coming to understand'; and, as my daughters might say, 'chilled out a bit'. If nothing else, writing this book has reminded me just how enjoyable it is to spend time working out new ideas with people.

📖 Further reading

Campbell, A., McNamara, O. and Gilroy, P. (2004) *Practitioner Research and Professional Development in Education*. London: Paul Chapman Publishing.

Mathematics Teaching: the journal of the Association of Teachers of Mathematics. This is available by subscription to the Association or through a local academic library. You can also access many articles online at www.atm.org.uk.

Mathematics in School and *Primary Mathematics*: the journals of the Mathematical Association. See www.m-a.org.uk, subscribe or access through a local library.

Assessment for Learning: available on the QCA website: www.qca.org.uk.

PHOTOCOPIABLE RESOURCES

This page is all about …

The key idea is …

This is how the idea works …

Watch out for …

Try practising on these examples …

Top tips to remember are …

Answers to examples are …

Author's note

Page 132 provides two examples of worksheets with no instructions (see page 81). The first example illustrates subtracting 9 from a 2 digit number and the second example illustrates multiplication by 5.

Page 133 shows an example of a 'completed' worksheet (see page 83). Note: the work completed by the 'child' models a misunderstanding of place value. Both the tens and ones digits of the multiplicand are multiplied as if they were ones. The exception is where the multiplier is a power of two, in which case a doubling method is used, accurately. It is possible to model many other common misconceptions.

$24 - 9 = \boxed{}$

$47 - 9 = \boxed{}$

$37 - \boxed{} = 28$

$\boxed{} - 9 = 72$

$1 \times 5 = \boxed{}$

$2 \times \boxed{} = 10$

$3 \times$

$\times 5 =$

$5 \qquad 25$

$6 \times 5 = \boxed{}$

$9 \times 5 = \boxed{}$

Multiplication

Work out the following ...

1.	**15 × 7**	$1 \times 7 = 7$ $5 \times 7 = 35$ $7 \times 35 = 42$ <u>42</u>
2.	**23 × 8**	23×8 $23 \times 2 = 46$ $46 \times 2 = 92$ $92 \times 2 = 184$ <u>184</u>
3.	**34 × 9**	$3 \times 9 = 27$ $4 \times 9 = 36$ $36 + 27 = 63$ <u>63</u>
4.	**58 × 4**	$58 \times 4 \ldots$ $58 \times 2 = 116$ $116 \times 2 = 232$ <u>232</u>
5.	**63 × 5**	$6 \times 5 = 30$ $3 \times 5 = 15$ $30 + 15 = 45$ <u>45</u>

Research Paper in Mathematics

Title:

Authors:

Abstract (summarise what you found out in one sentence):

Our Mathematical Analysis (explain what you did and how you explored the topic; show your mathematical ideas and give some examples):

Our Proof (explain why the reader should be convinced about your ideas):

Conclusion and Further Research Questions (write a concluding comment and identify any further questions that could be explored):

Contact Details (explain how people can contact you about your ideas):

Mathematical aspects of learning

Assessment grid for key mathematical concepts

Names	Generalisation	Proof	Conjecture	Isomorphism	Algorithm

(Adapted from Koshy, V. (2001) *Teaching Mathematics to Able Children*, London: David Fulton Publishers.)

Dispositions towards mathematics

Names	Curiosity	Creativity	Facts	Fluency	Skills

(Adapted from Koshy, V. (2001) *Teaching Mathematics to Able Children*, London: David Fulton Publishers.)

Photocopiable: *Interactive Maths Teaching in the Primary School*
© Paul Chapman Publishing, 2006, Nick Pratt

GLOSSARY OF TERMS

Appropriation Describing the way in which teachers can habitually take over children's responses to questions and use them for their own teaching rather than listening to what they have to say. See also (in)appropriation.

Classroom discourse (see also 'discourse') The particular discourse associated with the classroom. This will include the language of the classroom (objectives, groups, work etc.), the practices (ways of working and behaving) and the norms and expectations (ways of 'getting on' in the situation).

Complements (to 10 or 100 etc.) The 'complement' to 10 is the number that pairs up with another number to total 10. For example, if I have 4, its complement to 10 is 6. If I have 47, its complement to 100 is 53.

Discourse The talk, practices, norms and expectations often implicit in a situation and which strongly affect the way of behaving in that context.

Framework The folder sent to all teachers at the initiation of the NNS outlining key features and containing key objectives, sample planning for schools and a list of examples of objectives in each year group. Updated in 2006 under the Primary National Strategy.

(In)appropriation A word created for the purposes of this book to describe occasions when a teacher's appropriation of a child's response is inappropriate for effective interaction.

Mathematical discourse (see also 'discourse') The particular discourse associated with the subject of mathematics. This will include mathematical language (sum, integer, reason etc.), practices (problem solving, reasoning, finding efficient methods) and norms and expectations (tackling problems in certain ways, justifying explanations).

Multiplicand The first number in a multiplication problem, on which the multiplier acts to produce the product. For example, in the problem 12 x 8 = 96, the multiplicand is 12, the multiplier is 8 and the product is 96.

NNS National Numeracy Strategy

Plenary The word used to describe coming together as a class for the final ten minutes or so of a lesson to discuss the ideas raised in the main part of a lesson. 'Plenaries' are strongly recommended by the PNS, though often the hardest element of the lesson to do well according to inspection evidence.

PNS Primary National Strategy. An overarching strategy for primary education in England which subsumed the NNS and NLS.

Polygon Any 2D, straight-sided, closed (i.e. joined-up sides) shape – note, sides must not cross each other. For example, all the quadrilaterals and pentagons etc. are polygons, but the circle is not (sides are not straight).

Polyhedron Any closed (no gaps in it) 3D shape made entirely of polygons (i.e. all faces are flat).

Practice What teachers actually do in the classroom.

Theory The knowledge and ideas that teachers hold about their actions. Theory can help us to understand how and why we act the way we do, and what the implications for this action are.

REFERENCES

Ainley, J., Pratt, D. and Hansen, A. (2006) 'Connecting engagement and focus in pedagogic task design', *British Educational Research Journal*, 32(1), 23–38.

Alexander, R. (2000) *Culture and Pedagogy: International Comparisons in Primary Education*. Oxford: Blackwell Publishers.

Black, P. and Wiliam, D. (1998) *Inside the Black Box: Raising Standards Through Classroom Assessment*. London: King's College.

Brown, M. (1999) 'Swings of the pendulum', in I. Thompson (Ed.), *Issues In Teaching Numeracy In Primary Schools*. Buckingham: Open University Press.

Brown, M., Millett, A., Bibby, T. and Johnson, D. (2000) 'Turning our attention from the what to the how: the National Numeracy Strategy', *British Educational Research Journal*, 26(4), 457–71.

Brown, M., Askew, M., Millett, A. and Rhodes, V. (2003) 'The key role of educational research in the development and evaluation of the national numeracy strategy', *British Educational Research Journal*, 29(5), 655–72.

Burns, C. and Myhill, D. (2004) 'Interactive or inactive? A consideration of the nature of interaction in whole class teaching', *Cambridge Journal of Education*, 34(1), 35–49.

DES (1982) *Mathematics Counts*. London: HMSO.

DES (1989) *Mathematics in the National Curriculum*. London: HMSO.

DFE (1995) *Mathematics in the National Curriculum*. London: HMSO.

DfEE (1998) *The Implementation of the National Numeracy Strategy – The Final Report of the Numeracy Task Force*. London: DfEE.

DfEE (1999a) *The National Numeracy Strategy; Framework for Teaching Mathematics from Reception to Year 6*. London: DfEE.

DfEE (1999b) *Guide for your professional development: Book 1. The daily mathematics lesson*. London: DfEE.

DfEE (1999c) *Mathematical Vocabulary*. London: DfEE.

Fielker, D. (1997) *Extending Mathematical Ability Through Whole Class Teaching*. London: Hodder and Stoughton.

Hardman, F., Smith, F., Mroz, M. and Wall, K. (2003) 'Interactive whole class teaching in the national literacy and numeracy strategies', Paper presented at The British Educational Research Association Annual Conference, Heriot-Watt University, Edinburgh, 11–13 September.

Koshy, V. (2001) *Teaching Mathematics to Able Children*. London: David Fulton Publishers.

Mercer, N. (2000) *Words and Minds*. London: Routledge.

NCC (1989) *Mathematics Non-Statutory Guidance*. York: National Curriculum Council.

Pimm, D. (1987) *Speaking Mathematically: Communication in Mathematics Classrooms*. London: Routledge and Kegan Paul Ltd.

Sfard, A., Nesher, P., Streefland, L., Cobb, P. and Mason, J. (1998) 'Learning Mathematics Through Conversation: Is it as Good as They Say?', *For the Learning of Mathematics*, 18(1), 41–51, Ontario, Canada, FLM Publishing Association.

Stewart, I. (1996) *From Here to Infinity: A Guide to Today's Mathematics*. Oxford: Oxford University Press.

Wells, G. (1987) *The Meaning Makers: Children Learning Language and Using Language to Learn*. London: Hodder and Stoughton.

INDEX